SUPERACHIEVERS: PORTRAITS OF SUCCESS

Dedication

This book is dedicated to all those people who strive for excellence in their daily lives. They are the ones who use the gifts of wisdom, motivation, and encouragement.

SUPERACHIEVERS: PORTRAITS OF SUCCESS

by GERHARD GSCHWANDTNER

PERSONAL SELLING POWER, INC.
Fredericksburg, Virginia

© 1991 *by*
PERSONAL SELLING POWER, INC.
Fredericksburg, Virginia

Library of Congress Cataloging in Publication Data
Main entry under title:

Superachievers: portraits of success.

Bibliography: p.
1. Success—Case studies—Addresses, essays, lectures.
2. Interviews—United States. I. Gschwandtner, Gerhard.
BJ1611.2.S83   1984   158′.1   84–3391

ISBN 0-13-876384-4

10 9 8

Printed in the United States of America

Acknowledgments

No creative effort springs forth from a void. Countless influences, impressions, struggles, and conflicts go into any finished work. This book, *Superachievers,* began with Jim Savage of the Zig Ziglar Corporation. It was he who suggested that I put the interviews into book form. I wish to thank him, along with all of the superachievers, for their time, consideration, and attention. Were it not for the combined life wisdom of Mary Kay, Dr. Norman Vincent Peale, Zig Ziglar, Dr. Denis Waitley, Dr. David Burns, Gerard I. Nierenberg, Venita VanCaspel, Art Linkletter, Dr. Wayne Dyer, Senator Sam Ervin Jr., and Dr. Ken Cooper, this book would not exist. It is, in fact, a testimonial to their enduring spirit and dedication. Suzy Sutton's generosity in sharing two of her best interviews and insights has been invaluable.

The many facets of production involved in a book of this sort are complex. Willard Downes, the artist responsible for the fine portraits, has been generous with his time and energy. Barbara Crookshanks has likewise spent countless hours editing copy for the original interviews and the finished book. My wife Laura, who designed the book, suggested many of the interview subjects, and also discussed theories, concepts, and contradictions with me.

Special thanks go to the entire staff of *Personal Selling Power;* this book has been a joint project and I am grateful for their diligent efforts.

Gerhard Gschwandtner

Table of Contents

Warning to the Reader

You can't become successful without first finding an answer to the question, "What creates success?"

As you read the portraits of these twelve Super-perachievers, do not yield to the temptation to let them answer that question for you. Also, don't try to pick out the raisins. Instead, search for the roots of the grapevine.

Many people believe that they can become successful by imitating the successful habits of Superachievers, but this is putting the cart before the horse. Imitation is limitation. People who imitate carry only images of the end product of success in their minds. They stick a picture of yachts or Cadillacs on their mirrors and overlook the crucial difference between the fruits of success and the roots of success. They see the end but not the beginning.

Success begins with the development of your own personal success philosophy. It is your philosophy about your health that guides and shapes your attitudes toward your body. It is your philosophy about money that expands and improves your ability to make money. It is your philosophy about negotiation that creates and builds the tools you use in the negotiation process.

In the interviews with these Superachievers, you will

find inspiring accounts of how they struggled to define, adjust, and redefine their own personal success philosophies until they reached their ultimate success.

Look at successful business executives; listen to their advice. You'll find that they spend countless hours and dollars to find the answer to the simple question, "What business are we in?" They know that the answer to this key question creates a stable platform from which all corporate decisions can be made to ensure consistency, flexibility, growth, and success.

A business lacking a clearly defined statement of purpose is doomed to fail. Translated to a personal level, if you have failed to consciously define a philosophy of success, you have unconsciously defined a philosophy of failure. This is true simply because, if your life is not guided by philosophy, it will be guided by fantasy. Many people use fantasies or daydreams to protect themselves from reality. They overlook the fact that daydreaming simply amounts to avoiding reality altogether. Well-defined success philosophies will lead to great success in reality, whereas fantasies of success will lead only to greater illusions.

Let go of your daydreaming and you will become successful. In many instances, as you will read in these interviews, reality will far exceed the daydreams you are settling for now.

One more word of caution: Don't limit your success philosophy to a single area. A business can be run on a single statement of purpose; your life cannot. A single success philosophy will only get you success in one area. Success in one area will make you an achiever, not a Superachiever.

As you read each interview, you will be able to examine, revise, upgrade, and redefine your personal philosophies in such important areas as physical health (Dr. Kenneth H. Cooper), money (Venita VanCaspel), motivation (Zig Ziglar), negotiation (Gerard I. Nierenberg), mental health (Dr. David Burns), and many more.

Definitions

achieve

1. To bring to a successful end; to accomplish.
2. To get or attain by effort; to achieve victory.
3. To bring about an intended result; to accomplish some purpose.

super

A formal element occurring in loan words from Latin (*supersede*). Used, with the meaning "above," "beyond," in the formation of compound words with second elements of any origin (*superman, superhighway*).

Learn from the success philosophies of these Superachievers, stop dreaming about success, take the first step, and define your own success philosophies. They will become your personal foundation to success.

Keep in mind that it takes no more energy to reach success than to reach failure. This book tells you how to focus your energies to become a Superachiever.

Before you read this book, let me warn you again: If you have failed to consciously define a philosophy of success, you have unconsciously defined a philosophy of failure. It's up to you to choose, decide, and then succeed.

1

SUCCESS

Turning the Dream into Reality

"The only place where success comes before work," explains a hand-painted sign in a training center for junior athletes in Fredericksburg, Virginia, "is in the dictionary."

But work alone does not always lead to success.

Before you can begin working toward success, you need to (1) define what success means to you, and (2) decide on the action steps leading to success.

To learn how the readers of *Personal Selling Power* define success and to understand more about their action steps, we interviewed a number of men and women across the nation. You'll find a summary of their answers and insights on the following pages.

In retrospect, I realize that the most difficult task is to define clearly what success means to you. It is also the most overlooked task. Many people tend to underestimate the importance of defining success for themselves and end up copying someone else's definition.

On the surface, the question about the meaning of success appears easy. It is not. During the past seventy years, more than 1200 books have been written on the subject of success. Many of them define success and attempt to explain how to reach it.

Upon closer examination, you'll find that neither a book nor any other person can answer accurately for you what you really want for yourself out of life. And without an answer to this question, you'll have little chance of getting what you want.

Although the action steps for success can be drawn from many sources, the meaning of success can be drawn from only one source: yourself.

The Superachievers I've interviewed have consciously defined success based on sound self-knowledge. They recognize the simple truth that success draws its meaning from self-knowledge. For success to become meaningful to you, you must look within. It cannot be found outside yourself.

Lack of self-knowledge is thus the main obstacle to finding the meaning of success and to finding success meaningful. Lack of self-knowledge becomes the major source of disappointment as people reach success based on someone else's definition.

Self-knowledge comes from searching for answers to questions like:

- What do I want to achieve in life?
- How will I measure my achievements?
- What are my talents and capabilities?
- What will I invest or trade for becoming successful?
- How will success change and improve my life?
- How will other people benefit from my achievements?
- What does success really mean to me?

As we grow, our self-knowledge changes, and revisions and updates become necessary. A rigid definition of success will always inhibit growth. Maximum flexibility will always translate into maximum potential for success.

Self-knowledge holds not only the key to defining your success philosophy but also the key to building a strong commitment to your action plans.

If your definition of success is based on clear self-knowledge, your commitment will be in your heart, and no obstacle will hold you back. If, however, your definition of success is merely adopted from the outside, your commitment will be only in your head, and you are bound to lose it the very moment you encounter resistance.

This chapter will provide useful ideas for defining success and for choosing your action plans.

"If a man wants his dream to come true, he must wake up!" said one reader of Personal Selling Power.

To uncover the secrets of success, the editors contacted ninety-two sales and marketing executives around the country. Although they asked only four simple questions, at first the answers very much resembled the more than 3 billion combinations of Rubik's Cube.

But after hours of study and analysis, they discovered four basic ways to measure success, the two major reasons why people fail, and the five most important steps leading to success.

The following questions were asked in the telephone survey:

1. What is your measure of success?
2. What is your measure of failure?
3. What is the most important ability or skill leading to success?
4. Why do people fail?

How would you answer these? Then think of your company. How would your sales team answer these questions?

THE MEASURE OF SUCCESS

Chances are that the answers will fall into four basic categories:

Having Something

"Money!"

"For me it's having a comfortable life-style, a big house."

"Owning a boat, a truck, a couple of cars . . . having a wife and three kids."

Experiencing a Special Feeling

"Feeling that I did a good job, that I helped that customer."

"Loving my work."

"If I wake up in the morning with a smile . . . I know that I'm happy."

"The feeling of self-satisfaction."

"The feeling that I can relate well, that I can get very excited about my product."

Setting Goals and Reaching Them

"I measure success by the ability to set goals, to manage the obstacles on the way to my goals, and also by the results I get."

"Achieving what I want for myself."

"Whether or not I reach my sales quota . . . the one I set for myself."

"It's important to align personal goals with company goals. If I can do that, then I consider myself successful."

Following a Mission

"We all have a mission in life. We have to find what it is and work hard at fulfilling that mission."

"My aim is to do things that are worthwhile, that influence other people's lives in a positive way . . . making their lives better."

"My measure is whether I leave this world in better shape than I found it."

Many survey respondents shared their personal philosophies about success. Here are some points to ponder:

"We are either successful in reaching our goals or successful in creating the illusion that success is something we don't really need."

"I guess today fewer people truly want professional success. There are a lot more who are pursuing only one of two short-term goals: one is looking good, the other feeling good. We've entered a new ballgame."

The fact that salespeople measure their success in one of four basic ways can be useful in motivating your sales force.

For example, when a new sales campaign is introduced, you can point out how this new goal can be translated into:

1. New opportunities for "having more."
2. Additional chances for experiencing that "special feeling."
3. A unique challenge to set and reach new goals.
4. Another chance to pursue an important mission.

As a salesperson, you may consider identifying your client's measure of success. The question itself can lead to a productive conversation about the client's true goals and motivations, an invaluable source of information you can use for a successful close.

THE REASONS FOR FAILING

The second part of the survey was designed to identify the sources of failure. Here are the two major reasons why people fail.

Lack of Clear Goals

"Many people have dreams but can't decide on which one to pursue."

"If you don't have a goal, you become lazy, you get bored and forget what you want."

"They don't write down what they want to get out of life. If you want to succeed, you have got to have a plan."

Difficulties with Self-Motivation

"When I can't motivate myself, let's say after I've lost a sale, then I feel like a failure. That low point is sometimes the reason for losing other sales."

"It's either the fear of failure or the fear of success that prevents people from doing what they are capable of. I am no exception to that rule."

"I never seem to get all the things done that I want to get accomplished during one day. The backlog of paperwork, unfinished business, forgotten telephone calls . . . that's demotivating to me."

Many respondents admitted that it is difficult to keep focused on success at all times; also, during those moments when they lost sight of their goals, they consistently felt their motivation was at its lowest level.

Some could not think of specific reasons for failure. One insurance sales rep said, "I don't think about it, I don't plan for it, and I don't fail."

But what steps do we need to take to become successful? Below are the combined thoughts, ideas, and suggestions of *Personal Selling Power*'s readers and editors.

FIVE STEPS TO SUCCESS

1. Find Out What You Really Want

Mark Spitz was quoted as saying, several months after retiring, "The most difficult transition I had to make from athletics to everyday life was from knowing what I was going to do to not knowing."

Success depends on your ability to pursue a single goal. This means putting many other options on hold.

Artur Rubinstein was once approached by a young lady, who exclaimed in admiration, "I wish I could play the piano like you!" He replied, "If you're willing to practice six to eight hours a day and committed to invest many years of concentrated effort, your wish may come true!"

If you have a clear understanding of what you want, you will be successful. One sales executive replied to the question "What is your measure of success?" with this surprising description of what he wanted: "My measure of success is to have a new twenty-eight-foot cabin cruiser with five berths by October 31 next year. By January 1 next year, I plan on having $18,000 saved for this purchase."

You can guess how high his chances are for reaching his goal—compared to someone who'd say, "I guess I'd like to own a boat . . . someday . . . "

The cloudier your image of success, the greater your struggle in reaching what you want.

Begin your search for what you really want today!

2. Put Your Goals in Writing

Many people write wills to determine how to distribute their valuable estates among their loved ones.

Why not put your goals in writing, so you can clearly determine how valuable the rest of your life will be?

Based on sound economic principles, you can say that your future represents an asset that increases in value every single day. Isn't that a good enough reason to protect your life's interest with a solid plan for success?

Consider writing on a single page:

1. What do I want?
2. How will I get there?
3. What help do I need?
4. How will I measure what I've accomplished?

Once you've developed your plan for success, begin by investing every single future day toward the realization of your goal.

Here's a terrific day-by-day time management system that will help you to get what you want. At the start of each day, make a list of the six most important things you have to do. Rank these in order of their priority. Then begin with the first item on the list. Cross it off when you've completed the task.

Remember, if you have your plan for success only in your head, it's not worth the paper it's written on.

3. Check How Well You've Performed

Sometimes you may have trouble learning from your experiences. The difficulty lies in separating yourself from your plan and your results.

If your plan didn't work out, there is no reason to conclude that you are incompetent. If your plan fails, it's the plan that failed, not you.

Many salespeople avoid reviewing their performances because they secretly think, "What's the use of looking back? There's no point. I don't want to know." Why don't they want to know? They're afraid that the conclusion might be, "I'm no good." This erroneous thinking pattern prevents them from appraising the situation objectively.

If you accept the fact that you can't predict all possible variables in a plan and that mistakes can be viewed as a source of learning, you'll be able to commit yourself to personal growth and professional success.

Develop your own performance review system.

1. List your accomplishments.
2. List the unsolved problems.
3. Develop a revised plan of action.

Remember, you are not your plan. The only mistake you can make is not to learn from your experience.

4. Enjoy Reviewing the Benefits of Success

A vice-president of a large insurance company said with excitement in her voice, "Every morning I wake up with a 'success attack.' I can't wait to get out and do my work and pursue my goals!"

She was filled with enthusiasm because she knew what she wanted and she intended to fully enjoy the benefits of her success.

The sales manager whose goal is to get a twenty-eight-foot cabin cruiser said, "I carry a three-by-five card. On the front, I taped a picture of the boat; on the back I wrote the benefits of reaching my goal: (1) having more fun with my family, (2) exploring wild life, planning exciting trips, and (3) meeting new people and making new friends."

Review the benefits of your success. It's the key to self-motivation. As long as the benefits of reaching your goals outweigh the benefits of maintaining the status quo, you'll be able to experience many success attacks and keep the fire of enthusiasm burning within you.

5. Work Smarter

"Unless you apply your energies in a skillful and methodical way, you're stuck with a bunch of daydreams. It's the doer who gets the job done, not the dreamer," explained a successful New York advertising salesman.

Elbert Hubbard wrote in 1927, "Do your work with your whole heart and you will succeed—there is so little competition."

But how can you do your work with your whole heart? It's simple. Every job has three built-in obstacles. The first is within the job, the second is within yourself, and the third is with other people. Working smarter means removing these obstacles. But how?

Do the job and press on. Keep your eyes focused on the job (in front of you) and your mind's eye focused on success (inside you).

Work on yourself. Manage your moods. Freud once said, "A man with a toothache cannot be in love." We could translate this into, "A sales rep who doesn't manage his or her moods can't persuade a customer."

Mood management requires working on your attitude toward yourself. A negative attitude often starts with self-rejection and can easily end in self-defeat.

Increase your self-esteem and self-acceptance. Your potential for success rises proportionally to your self-esteem.

Learn to work with others. Zig Ziglar, one of the nation's top motivators, promises, "You can get everything in life you want, if you help enough other people get what they want."

To succeed, you need other people's help. Maintain an open attitude toward the world. You can't walk around with a closed attitude and expect the world to be open to you.

These five steps sound so simple, yet they are so difficult to keep in mind. More than 2000 years ago, when Euclid was explaining the principles of geometry to the king of

Egypt, his patron inquired whether the knowledge could not be obtained more easily. "Sir," said Euclid, "there is no royal road to learning."

This statement is still true today. There is no royal road to either wisdom or success. The path to success is not for kings alone. It's open to you and me. But remember, if you want your dream to come true, you must wake up.

KEY IDEAS TO REMEMBER

1. If your life is not guided by philosophy, it will be guided by fantasy.

2. If you have failed to consciously define a philosophy of success, you have unconsciously defined a philosophy of failure.

3. The clearer your definition of success, the greater your chances of reaching success. If you fail to define success, you can never hope to reach it.

4. The action steps to success can be drawn from many sources; the meaning of success can be drawn from only one source—yourself.

5. Maximum flexibility in your pursuit of success will translate into maximum potential for success.

Now please complete the Action Plan on the following page.

MY ACTION PLAN FOR SUCCESS

1.

2.

3.

4.

5.

2

Portrait of Persuasion:

RONALD REAGAN

Though history may tell a tale of great accomplishments, the key to Ronald Reagan's guiding philosophy to success can be found engraved on a simple plaque placed unobtrusively on his desk in the Oval Office.

"There is no limit to what a man can do or where he can go if he doesn't mind who gets the credit."

When I researched Ronald Reagan's personal selling power, I was impressed by the mastery this man has over his opponents. There is much to learn here. It is certainly true that Ronald Reagan has had and continues to have enormous success in dealing with people.

When I wrote this analysis, Mr. Reagan was in the early stages of his presidency. He has had ups and downs since then, but he seems to have emerged strong and confident. His persuasive techniques continue to impress me. His use of body language is masterful. He knows how to disarm the other fellow without either weakening his position or alarming the other side.

Disarming others is the beginning of any sale or negotiation.

Ronald Reagan's personal selling power has led to an impressive record of legislative success. He gets the job done by disarming and persuading, while letting others get the credit.

From the most humble beginnings, this man has risen to the highest office in the land. Ronald Reagan's father was a shoe salesman, and his mother coached a local drama group. He is the personification of the American Dream come true. For years he lectured from coast to coast on the values of the free enterprise system, thus rekindling the legacy of the nation's founders.

I dismissed the temptation of requesting a personal interview with Ronald Reagan for two reasons. First, this personal profile was planned and developed during *Personal Selling Power*'s first year of publication when its readership was fairly small. Second, I felt that the president could contribute more to this portrait by letting his actions speak for him.

RONALD REAGAN'S PERSONAL SELLING POWER

Ronald Reagan has the smiling confidence of a man who has been before an audience for nearly half a century. Before he says his first word, he has begun a successful sale. His relaxed appearance, his sparkling eyes, the sincere smile and open body language show his belief in himself and his ability to sell.

What are the secrets of his repeated successes, achieved—more often than not—over what seemed to be overwhelming odds?

"His greatest skill is his ability to communicate an idea or emotion," is the way New York Times *correspondent Robert Lindsey sums it up in the book* Reagan, The Man, The President.

Ronald Reagan is inspirational, dramatic, and a super salesman. No matter what political views you endorse, Reagan's personal selling power has proven effective for too long to be ignored by professional salespeople. In this chapter we'll examine how three separate professional and personal qualities have helped Ronald Reagan to outsell everyone else.

The Power of Using Stories

Like many successful salespeople, Ronald Reagan uses short stories to illustrate political (selling) points. Specialists in the art of persuasion concede that the storytelling process is mysterious and little understood. Some psychologists claim that we tend to reexperience a sense of childhood wonder and amazement when listening to stories, a fact that the adult storyteller knowingly uses to sell his or her ideas.

House Speaker Tip O'Neil was quoted as saying, "He's always got a disarming story. I don't know where he gets them, but he's always got them. He calls up: 'Tip, you and I are political enemies only until six o'clock. It's four o'clock, now; can we pretend it's six o'clock?' How can you dislike a guy like that?"

On the campaign circuit, Reagan used a brilliant story to sell his audience on the need to reduce the size of government: "There are now 2½ million federal employees. No one knows what they all do. One congressman found out what one of them does. This man sits at a desk in Washington. Documents come to him each morning. He reads them, initials them, and passes them on to the proper agency. One day a document arrived that he wasn't supposed to read, but he read it, initialed it, and passed it on. Twenty-four hours later it arrived back at his desk with a memo attached that said, 'You weren't supposed to read this. Erase your initials, and initial the erasure.'"

When Reagan tells a story, his greatest strength is in the mastery of his voice. He is able to skillfully catch the right tone, and his voice sometimes breaks when he tells an emotional story of heroism.

In his inaugural address he moved millions with these words describing Martin Treptow, a World War I soldier. "We are told that on his body was found a diary. On the flyleaf under the heading 'My Pledge,' he had written these words: 'America must win this war. Therefore I will work, I will save, I will sacrifice, I will endure. I will fight cheerfully and do my utmost, as if the issue of the whole struggle depended on me alone.'"

Reagan's previous acting experience has helped him to learn how to inject his own true emotions into each story he tells. As Constantin Stanislavski, the world-famous director, wrote in his book *An Actor Prepares*, "The great actor should be full of feeling, and especially he should feel the thing he is portraying. He must feel an emotion not only once or twice while he's studying his part, but every time he plays it."[1]

This is a lesson that applies equally well to selling.

The Power of Firm and Friendly Attitudes

Top salespeople consistently show two personality characteristics: the capacity to be firm *and* to be friendly. On the surface, these attitudes may be present in every salesperson—but not in equal measure. Salespeople who are too firm may bulldoze through a sale, annoying customers and causing unnecessary cancellations. Salespeople who are too friendly will get along fine with the customer but may lack the inner strength and fail to ask for the order.

Ronald Reagan expresses both qualities and knows how to use them in equal measure. On the friendly side, he's able to be very charming, pleasant, and personable; on the firm side, he can show his consistency in pursuing his conservative political views.

These qualities have a persuasive effect on people from all walks of life, here and abroad. After a meeting with Reagan, King Hussein of Jordan described the president as warm, interested, a man of great integrity, with a willingness to listen and to work. Caspar Weinberger commented that every foreign head of state has come away from Reagan very impressed and holding "a revised opinion of Reagan's strength as a leader."

He is firm in keeping his word, thus maintaining a high level of credibility. When he says he will take certain actions in a given situation, he follows through with no ifs, ands, or buts. He let the air traffic controllers know they would be fired if they went out on strike. They did . . . and they were.

In his November 1981 fight with Congress on the emergency spending bill, he said he would order a shutdown of the government if he wasn't satisfied with the bill.

They didn't meet his request, and he shut down the government.

The ability to be firm and friendly has helped Reagan to strike deals with legislators, to negotiate compromises with his political opponents, and to maintain a consistent positive public image.

Whichever side of Ronald Reagan emerges in a one-to-one selling situation, he approaches the opponent with a basic strategy: first disarm, then strike a deal.

In his dramatic victory during his campaign to get congressional sanction for the sale of AWACS radar planes, he held forty-eight private meetings with individual senators.

If the president didn't persuade someone the first time, he called him again and again. One senator who changed his opposing views after a private meeting with the president confessed, "I feel like I am going to need an arm transplant, it's been twisted so much."

The power of firm and friendly attitudes led to the AWACS sales success. In one instance Reagan appealed to an equally firm senator by looking him straight in the eye and saying, "How can I convince foreign leaders that I am in command if I cannot sell five airplanes?"

This last-ditch emotional appeal to patriotism did the trick. He got the last crucial vote and made the sale.

The Power of Simplicity

People love to buy from the sales rep who tells it like it is, simple and straightforward. Simplicity is an art, and it takes hard work. The following conversation between Woodrow Wilson and a reporter provides an example:

Reporter: "How long would it take you to prepare for a simple ten-minute speech?"

Wilson: "Two weeks."

Reporter: "How long for an hour speech?"

Wilson: "One week."

Reporter: "How long for a two-hour speech?"

Wilson: "I'm ready now."

Ronald Reagan is a master of simplifying communication and has an extraordinary talent for condensing ideas. The president's simplicity comes across in the following ways:

Simple language He stays clear of complex words or phrases. His audience does not need a dictionary to understand his thoughts. Like a good sales rep, he knows that life is too short to waste time with complicated language.

Simple mini-memos As governor of California, he developed a highly successful system for handing down decisions. After hearing out his subordinates' detailed recommendations, he would draft a concise one-page, four-paragraph summary of a problem with clear recommendations on how to solve it. His style initially drew criticism but got better results than that of the previous governor.

Simple persuasion techniques In his presidential campaign, he scored points with highly persuasive statements such as, "Recession is when your neighbor loses his job. Depression is when you lose yours. And recovery is

when Jimmy Carter loses his." Some of his simple but profound one-liners have created tremendous impact. For example, "How can we love our country and not love our countrymen?" Or, concerning the Panama Canal, "We built it, we paid for it, it's ours, and we are going to keep it."

Simple life philosophies Son of a shoe salesman, Ronald Reagan exudes an air of simple virtues. Haynes Johnson, a *Washington Post* writer, commented in a front-page editorial, "He lacks the arrogance or insecurities of some presidents. The presidency does not awe him; he's not uptight in the job. Those who have known him for years say he has changed hardly at all since entering the White House."

Ronald Reagan's knack for simplicity fools the casual observer. Critics have labeled his contagious optimism as "unrealistic cheerleading" and have described his willingness to listen as "he waits for others to advise him what to do; he is an endorser." But upon closer examination, many critics revise their opinion. One senator was quoted as saying, "The worry about Ronald Reagan when he came here, to judge from everything written and said about him, was whether he could last longer than nine to five without his cue cards. Well, he's certainly demolished that image."

What Reagan critics have overlooked is that pretending to be simple, less intelligent, or just playing dumb is part of his highly successful strategy. This is a persuasion technique that cannot coexist in an individual with an inflated self-image.

Simplicity is one of the most difficult skills leading to sales success. It's like the old saying, "The greatest truths are the simplest; and so are the greatest men."

Note

1. Printed with permission of Theatre Arts Books, New York, N.Y. Copyright © 1936 by Theatre Arts, Inc. Copyright © 1945 by Elizabeth R. Hapgood.

RONALD REAGAN: KEY IDEAS TO REMEMBER

1. There is no limit to what a person can do or where that person can go if he or she doesn't mind who gets the credit.

2. Top salespeople consistently show two personality characteristics: the capacity to be firm and the capacity to be friendly. Firmness ensures strength and consistency; friendliness leads to pleasant feelings. Both qualities need to be balanced to achieve maximum success.

3. The key principle to persuasion: First disarm your opponent, then strike a deal.

4. A good story, told with sincerity, will disarm, persuade, and sell an audience more effectively than facts or science ever will.

5. Simplicity is an art and takes hard work. Simplify your communication with others; condense your ideas. Life is too short to waste time with complicated language.

Now please complete the Action Plan on the following page.

MY ACTION PLAN FOR SUCCESS

1.

2.

3.

4.

5.

3

Portrait of Enthusiasm:

MARY KAY ASH

"Most people plan their vacations better than they plan their lives," says Mary Kay Ash. But, for the 170,000 salespeople in the Mary Kay organization, planning and goal setting are daily routine.

More women make more than $50,000 a year working for Mary Kay than in any other American company.

How do they do it? With enthusiasm, according to their mentor and the founder of this empire. She is America's number one saleswoman.

When I interviewed her I wondered how a simple personal philosophy like enthusiasm could create such fame and wealth. Her own enthusiasm spills over into thousands upon thousands of lives, like waves on the shore. They wash over each other, breaking down the sands of silent despair and building the cliffs of hope from which each woman can see her own horizon.

Mary Kay, more than any other woman of this century, represents a way for women to have their cake and eat it too. They have been able to fulfill their hopes and dreams while maintaining their dignity and an independence few had ever known before. Some who began their Mary Kay careers with the humblest of expectations have turned into top sales producers with six-figure incomes.

All of this is possible because of the guiding philosophy of the woman who started it all. Underlying the expression of enthusiasm, we see a woman who has a deep respect and understanding of her fellow women; their dreams are her dreams, their needs are also hers. At a time when women in sales were a rarity, Mary Kay was outperforming everyone. When she started her own company, against the advice of male experts, she made sure that she would never make the same assumptions about women that were made about her.

Today she has created a structure that gives women recognition, respect, and rewards.

During the interview she recalled her mother's philosophy: "If you give a man a fish, you feed him for a day, but if you teach him how to fish, you feed him for life." Mary Kay translated this guideline to feed and nurture thousands of women.

This philosophy will go on nurturing and feeding women long after Mary Kay has gone. Thus, the main objective of this philosophy is that others must be able to incorporate into their own lives what you have created through yours. What you create must improve those lives, and it must strengthen the bonds between people.

Mary Kay's enthusiasm is catching. The warmth she radiates is enveloping. To be in her presence makes one feel happy to be alive and glowing with the possibilities of the moment. She provides the structure, she sets the example, and she works hard. But, most of all, she lets you know, by all that she has done, that, "Honey, you can do it, too."

THE MAKEUP OF SALES SUCCESS

On Friday, September 13, 1963, Mary Kay Ash rented a storefront in Dallas to start her own company, Mary Kay Cosmetics.

Today, with sales approaching $600 million, she reflects on her humble beginnings. "One of my strongest motivations for starting was the determination to give women an opportunity that I was denied when I worked for others."

What Mary Kay created amounts to the unbelievable success story of America's most dynamic saleswoman.

In this interview with Personal Selling Power, *Mary Kay agreed to share the basic principles that account for her inner growth and sales success.*

PSP: The first thing that strikes me about your organization is the incredible enthusiasm that is expressed by your staff and your beauty consultants. How do you generate this enthusiasm?

Mary Kay: Somebody said, if you act enthusiastic, you will become enthusiastic. We try to generate enthusiasm by example.

PSP: What are some of the things you do to set the example?

Mary Kay: One of the things that I do personally is to keep some very good books on my bedside table that keep reminding me of what life is really all about. There are some days when you wake up and you really don't feel all that enthusiastic. I think that is true of every person.

PSP: It's true. What kind of books do you feel are helpful for those days?

Mary Kay: Besides the Bible, there are some very good motivational books, like Norman Vincent Peale's *The Power of Positive Thinking,* or one that inspired me and turned my life around at one time, *Think and Grow Rich* by Napoleon Hill; and of course *Psycho-Cybernetics* by Dr. Maxwell Maltz. All of these are not exactly the newest things on the market, but I keep reading the new ones and rereading the old ones. They keep me enthusiastic.

PSP: How do you help your salespeople to maintain their enthusiastic attitude?

Mary Kay: We have a lot to be enthusiastic about. But even back in those days when the success was small, we found ways to be enthusiastic about the things we did have. There are many ways to create enthusiasm in a group of salespeople. For example, we hold most sales meetings on Monday morning to challenge the "blue Monday syndrome." To me, Monday is a new beginning, a fresh start, and a new chance to do something positive. So, we start by singing songs. I feel very strongly about the effect of music and the action of singing. When you go to church, invariably the hymns are sung first. They create a very special feeling which leads to a positive attitude.

PSP: You've said that the test of a champion is "to be able to put on a happy face when deep down you are suffering over a serious problem." No matter how bad you feel, you must always go in enthusiastic-

ally. When your hostess says, "Hello, how are you?" the consultant must respond, "Wonderful, and how are you?" Isn't that a form of self-denial?

Mary Kay: No, I don't really think so. I think it has a therapeutic effect. For example, one of our directors, Rena Tarbet, has hit the Million Dollar Club for the third year. She has had cancer for seven years. Twenty-two days a month, she is on some kind of treatment that would normally put most of us in the hospital. Her doctor says, "Rena is living with cancer, not dying with it."

Just recently, one of her family members called me and they thought she was working too hard—she is now working on her fourth million, it is incredible—and I called her doctor to get his views. He said, "It is my opinion that it is that incredible, indomitable spirit of hers that keeps her going, and that is why she is where she is today, and I think she should be allowed to do anything she feels like doing."

PSP: Rena's work seems to prevent her from getting worse.

Mary Kay: Right. You heard about the man who said, "If I only went to work on the days I felt like it, I never would." If Rena stayed home and focused on the fact that she is ill, she would probably get worse.

PSP: Is it true that some of your salespeople start their workday at five o'clock in the morning?

Mary Kay: It's true. You know, if you get up at five o'clock three times a week, you'll gain an extra day. You need to try it a few times, because you'll realize a great feeling of satisfaction at eight o'clock in the morning when you've already finished what would have taken you six hours to do after eight o'clock because of the interruptions.

It's not infrequent that I get a call at five or six o'clock in the morning, and I always know that it is one of my eager beavers who is already up. An example is one of my top producers, Helen McVoy. She made $310,000 last year.

PSP: So, you feel you've had a head start while other people are still sleeping.

Mary Kay: Yes. By the time they get out of their beds, you've already finished half a day's work.

PSP: *It seems that you learned to work hard at a very early age.*

Mary Kay: I think I probably had a different situation from the average child. I don't ever remember my mother's being there to bake cookies or do any of the things that most mothers do, or help me with my lessons and tie my shoes. She had the very inconvenient situation of being away from me, and I think perhaps she felt a little guilty about not being able to be there to do the things that she thought that she should be doing. So, she used the telephone. You know that old saying, "If you give a man a fish, you feed him for a day, but if you teach him how to fish, you feed him for life." My mother applied that principle. Over the telephone, she would tell me exactly how to do every little thing that I needed to know as a child. She always would say, "Honey, you can do it," or "Anything anyone else can do, you can do better." I think that the reason she would constantly add, "You can do it," was because she wasn't really sure I could.

PSP: *In a way, your mother's expectations seem to have translated into your expectations of your people in the Mary Kay organization where you encourage others by saying, "You can do it, too."*

Mary Kay: Right. That's what we do on a constant, everyday basis.

PSP: *It's a very powerful principle.*

Mary Kay: It worked for me. And it's working today for a lot of people. I am amazed at how many people come up to me and say, "You know, I met you in Chicago and you took my hand and you looked in my eyes and you said, 'You know, I just know that you can do it.'"

PSP: *Do you feel that women need to be motivated differently from men?*

Mary Kay: In some ways, I think men are motivated more by money than women are. I've often heard men say,

"Why do you spend all this money on a mink coat? Why don't you just give them cash?" I don't think that women would be as motivated by cash as they would by the possibility of having a mink coat that they have dreamed about all their lives. If they received the cash, it probably would go for a dishwasher or something like that.

PSP: What do you feel is the number one motivator that women respond to?

Mary Kay: Recognition comes first, self-fulfillment second, and then third, I think, is pride.

PSP: Self-fulfillment would mean...

Mary Kay: Accomplishing something that probably their husbands didn't think they could do or maybe they themselves didn't think they could do.

PSP: In a way, you create a competitive situation that allows them to get recognized and feel fulfilled.

Mary Kay: Well, we've created a competitive situation, but we've removed all the dog-eat-dog jealousy factor and all the scratching somebody else's eyes out to get where you want to go.

PSP: What do you do to prevent that?

Mary Kay: In some of the companies that I was in, there was always a first, second, and third prize, and invariably there were always three hot shots in the company who would win those. So, what's the use of trying? We put everything on a plateau basis. In other words, if we have a contest, you know that it will take X number of dollars wholesale to get into that rank. You don't have to step on anybody to get the reward; you can all reach for it and get it. In essence, our salespeople compete with themselves.

PSP: Do you feel that this system leads to a better overall attitude among salespeople?

Mary Kay: Absolutely. We are talking about creating a go–give attitude. If you give the very best you have in whatever you do, the best will then come back to you in a kind of boomerang effect. It certainly has worked for me, and the more I give, the more it comes back. And yet, you don't ever think about it. I mean, I never think about that when I am giving, I'm going to get a whole lot back. That doesn't work. You give without any expectation of return.

PSP: *You also suggest to put God first, family second, and career third.*

Mary Kay: Right. If you put God first in your life, you don't have to worry about much else. Then, your family should come next. It is my opinion that if you make the most money in the whole world and in the process lose your husband and your children just for the dollar, then you've failed.

PSP: *Life would lose its meaning.*

Mary Kay: Yes, there are a lot of things more important than just making money.

PSP: *Managing a family and a career calls for a certain amount of organizational skills and good time management habits.*

Mary Kay: Yes, it does.

PSP: *What are some success principles that you've developed for yourself in this area?*

Mary Kay: Well, one of the most important principles that I ever learned is to write each evening the six most important things I have to do tomorrow. I also number them in the order of their importance. You need to make that decision, because a woman can walk into any room of the house and find six things that need to be done. By deciding what's most important, I can follow what I set out to do and don't get off on all kinds of tangents.

PSP: *Why six items and not ten or twelve?*

Mary Kay: You need to balance the number of tasks with your possibilities of completing them in the time available. If you would write down twenty-six items, you'd get frustrated and say, "I can't do all that," and end up doing nothing. But six things you can do. And then I always say, with a smile, "If you get those done, you can take the rest of the day off with my blessing."

PSP: *Do you always begin to work with a clean desk in the morning?*

Mary Kay: I usually start with a clean desk.

PSP: And when you finish the day?

Mary Kay: I take it all home.

PSP: The reading matter?

Mary Kay: Oh, I have it in nice little piles here. One is to read, one is to sign, and one is for dictation. I like to work on these things early in the morning while I'm real fresh. There is another little habit that applies to time management and organization. I've discovered that whatever is on top of your incoming mail, you take it and finish it. I don't go on to the second, no matter how enticing. Normally you tend to go through the pile and think, "Oh, here is an easy one, I'll do that one first," and, "I don't know the answer to this one, so I'll put it aside for awhile." My suggestion is: You tackle one thing at a time and finish it, no matter how difficult it is or how easy it is. You don't handle any piece of paper twice.

PSP: Sooner or later you'll have to make the decision anyway. So, it's better to make it now.

Mary Kay: Right, get it over with.

PSP: Doesn't it feel good to cross things off your list?

Mary Kay: Yes, I love it.

PSP: How do you deal with procrastination? I've heard that sometimes there is a little problem with follow-up calls.

Mary Kay: Yes. It is caused by fear of rejection when they think, "Oh, my goodness, that lady may not like it . . . maybe I couldn't answer her question. Maybe she's not at home.

PSP: Even though they may have the item on their list, this fear prevents them from completing the job.

Mary Kay: Yes.

PSP: How do you suggest they deal with it?

Mary Kay: Well, by discipline first of all. I suggest that they put aside one hour, put a sand-timer in front of them, and talk to one person every three minutes. Make that call and succinctly ask the questions that need to be asked, do whatever has to be done, and get off the phone to call the next person. Many consultants have a tendency to talk too long and talk for thirty-five minutes because they enjoy it. If she would keep these calls short and business-like, she would keep her business in fine shape and would keep her bookings and her production going. Our top producers say that an ounce of pink tickets (follow-up call reminders) is worth an ounce of gold.

PSP: You were once quoted as saying: "One intense hour is worth a dreamy day." What did you mean by that?

Mary Kay: Well, Parkinson's Law states that "work expands to fill the time available for it." If somebody called you from the airport saying, "We just arrived in town and we'll be there in half an hour," you'd get your spring cleaning done in thirty minutes, when you might have spent a whole day on it. Whatever length of time you have available for a project, like these follow-up calls, you get it done.

PSP: So if you don't develop sound time management principles, you won't be able to reach your goals.

Mary Kay: Right.

PSP: What are some of the success principles you use that apply to goal setting?

Mary Kay: Well, first of all, you're never going to get there if you don't know where you are going. I think most people plan their vacations better than they plan their lives.

PSP: So you recommend that they set realistic short-term and long-term goals?

Mary Kay: I think that short-term goals are more applicable. I know, for example, I find myself thinking in terms of what's going on today and the rest of this quarter. Richard Rogers (president of Mary Kay) is already thinking about 1985. As far as I am concerned, it's not ever going to happen.

By the way, Richard just brought in this picture of our new office complex that we are building on 177 acres. Almost every department will have its own building. It's like a little city with a lake in the center, a marina, and eventually we are even going to have a hotel.

PSP: *It sounds as if the success principles you've applied in your company since 1963 have helped you grow far beyond what you imagined you could do.*

Mary Kay: Well, I feel that God had a very important job to be done here. You know that I am a great-grandmother?

PSP: *Right.*

Mary Kay: So I realize that time is precious and that I don't have forever to do all these things. For this reason I am trying to set the concepts so that other Mary Kays can carry on long after I am gone.

PSP: *How do you think this will happen?*

Mary Kay: I think this will come about through my National Sales Directors, who, in essence, believe in everything I believe in, and who are where they are because they are almost stamped-out copies. I have just returned from a ten-day trip with the top ten nationals. Just being with them every day was an interesting experience—it was almost like looking into a mirror.

PSP: *It appears that one of your greatest contributions to the expansion of your company was to motivate a large number of people to use their own capabilities and to apply many of your proven success principles.*

Mary Kay: Yes, I think that is really true. I think that one of the greatest contributions we have made is to help people realize how great they really are and to reach their potential.

MARY KAY: KEY IDEAS TO REMEMBER

1. If you give the very best you have in whatever you do, the best will come back to you in a boomerang effect.

2. Write down each evening the six most important things you have to do the next day. By deciding what's most important, you can follow what you set out to do and not go off on tangents.

3. If you get up at five o'clock three times a week, you'll gain an extra day. Try it, and you'll realize the great feeling of satisfaction at eight o'clock in the morning when you've already finished what would have taken you six hours to do after eight o'clock because of the interruptions.

4. Don't handle any piece of paper twice. Whatever is on the top of your incoming mail, take it and finish it. Don't go on to the second, no matter how enticing.

5. People plan their vacations better than they plan their lives.

Now please complete the Action Plan on the following page.

MY ACTION PLAN FOR SUCCESS

1.

2.

3.

4.

5.

4

Portrait of Independence:

DR. WAYNE DYER

Independence is the key to Dr. Wayne Dyer's guiding philosophy. In thoughts, decisions, and actions, he sets his own course and then follows it to the end.

His incredible energy is what impressed me the first time I spoke with him. His words come at you fast, expressed with certainty and a lack of restraint that sweep you up and almost bowl you over. He never pressures; he listens intently but refuses to allow someone else's twisted thinking to interfere with the flow of his life.

He decided early in his life that if there was something he wanted, he must get it for himself. From his background and upbringing, no one would have predicted the overwhelming success and recognition that have found their way to his door. He has always been on the move, never giving up the search for those things in life that were worth wanting.

If the concept of the no-limit person has never touched your life, then you are one of the few exceptions. Dr. Dyer began that movement and has popularized the philosophy that says that you are ultimately responsible for yourself and your actions. You can determine your own thoughts and feelings. You can decide how to manage any thought or dream, a concept that makes you the sole master of your destiny.

After speaking with him, I found that my energy level soared to a new high for about a week. I wondered exactly what had gone on and how I could reproduce that feeling in a lasting way.

What I discovered was that I was reacting to more than Dr. Dyer's energy. Talking with him released my own locked-up possibilities. I realized that the energy you spend worrying and wondering about success and failure will simply reduce the energy needed for the task. The no-limit person can decide to be concerned no longer with thoughts and feelings that have been imposed by the outside world, thus focusing his or her energies to get the job done.

Most of us have been taught that competition is the only way to measure success and failure. For some of us, it is the only way to keep going and to perform. But according to Dr. Dyer's philosophy, competition is the major reason for giving up control of our lives.

"Suppose you are going for a walk," he illustrates with an everyday example. "If you are a competitive person, the walking becomes a test. If you measure your walk in terms of someone else's standards, then you can't just stop when you feel like it and look at a flower. You can't just go for a mediocre walk. You can't really feel the wind on your face. No. You have to take a better walk than someone else."

Dr. Dyer recommends that you don't walk with anyone else's legs and that you don't measure your performance by using anyone else's standards. On your journey to success, you must use your own legs, your own eyes, and your own thoughts and feelings. No one can be in control of your life but you. No one can set the standards for your success but you. To succeed, simply put one foot in front of the other and advance confidently in the direction of your own dreams.

SPACE-AGE SELLING PSYCHOLOGY

Dr. Wayne Dyer, supersalesman, worldwide lecturer, and TV personality, is the number one best-selling author of such life-changing books as Your Erroneous Zones, Pulling Your Own Strings, The Sky's the Limit, *and* Gifts from Eykis.

Only a few years ago, he boldly introduced the concept of the no-limit person. He proposed to cut through the tangle of negative emotions, habits, and obligations that bind us to the ground.

In this interview, Dr. Dyer offers an eye-opening message of hope, freedom, and challenge, as well as a clear picture of his inner blueprint for success.

PSP: Do you consider yourself a good salesman?

Dr. Dyer: I do. I have been called one of the top salesmen in the publishing field. People say I am a terrific book salesman. However, I have never made a conscious effort to sell anything in my life, and yet I know that I am an excellent salesman.

PSP: What did you do to become an excellent salesman?

Dr. Dyer: I achieved inner serenity. I don't believe in pushing my products on anyone else. I think I am a good salesman because when I'm on the air, I just sell myself. I talk common sense. I talk from a perspective of being someone that other people would want to hear and know more about. And as a result—and that's even done unconsciously—people then want to go out and buy my books to know more about what I do.

PSP: You say it's done unconsciously. What subconscious message do you communicate?

Dr. Dyer: You simply sell yourself. You believe in who you are and what you do. I believe in the concept of modeling. You have to model whatever it is you're asking somebody else to become.

PSP: So, in selling, the first product you have to be concerned with is yourself?

Dr. Dyer: Right. In my latest book, *Gifts from Eykis,* I use a quote from Thoreau describing what I mean: "If one advances confidently in the direction of his own dreams, and endeavors to live the life which he has imagined, he will meet with a success unexpected in common hours." If you're a person who really, truly believes in yourself and the possibility of reaching your dreams, then that will come through and other people will want more of you. This also applies to the products you're associated with.

PSP: You seem to describe charisma.

Dr. Dyer: Yes, I think of it as an enthusiasm for life. It is a genuine excitement of who you are and what you are doing. Translated into selling, it means that you communicate to other people that you really care about them as people, rather than as buyers of your product.

PSP: Could you tell us about your first major sale and how you have applied this technique?

Dr. Dyer: I think my biggest sale was my book, *Your Erroneous Zones.* When I met with the publisher's editorial vice-president to talk about the sale of my manuscript, I realized that he had just experienced a personal setback in his life. He was upset about it. I stayed in his office for four hours, and we never discussed the book all afternoon. We talked about a problem that we both had faced in our lives. I talked to him from a perspective of a caring person. I suspended all my desire to get my book published. I was just doing what seemed to make sense to me at that moment, trusting my inner instincts. The next day he called and told me they were going to publish my book.

PSP: It appears that your ability to suspend your preoccupation with selling your book was the key to the sale.

Dr. Dyer: Yes, human love, the ability to reach out to a person, is the greatest sales technique in the world.

PSP: In your opinion, what are the key characteristics of an effective salesperson?

Dr. Dyer: I think first and foremost of someone who has positive self-values, self-worth, self-esteem. That is at the very top. When you don't have that, then all of the other things don't make any difference. In addition, you should have the ability to communicate a feeling of enthusiasm, a feeling of excitement about who you are and what you're doing—being able to live up to what you're selling, being a model, being flexible, and having a sense of humor.

PSP: What are the keys to improving your relationship with a customer or prospect?

Dr. Dyer: It all boils down to what they need and

what I can provide. It means shifting your concern from problems to solutions. Solution-oriented thinking comes from caring and loving. You have to see things through the eyes of the other person. You should be so involved in helping another human being that your own needs became unimportant.

PSP: How about the problem customer? What do you feel are the most significant barriers?

Dr. Dyer: I honestly believe they are all within ourselves. To me, there are no barriers, only challenges.

PSP: Have you ever counseled salespeople on an individual basis?

Dr. Dyer: I've done a lot of that.

PSP: What do you feel are the most common obstacles that salespeople seem to put in their own way?

Dr. Dyer: The biggest one is the fear of failure, equating their performance on the job with who they are as a person.

PSP: What do you mean by that?

Dr. Dyer: In other words, they are telling themselves, "If I make the sale, I can be happy. If I don't make the sale, I can't be happy."

PSP: Do you ever experience the fear of failure when you write a book or appear on national television?

Dr. Dyer: No. I learned something very important. When I write, I write for myself. When I first started writing, I submitted 100 articles that were rejected. Anybody in his right mind would have said, "Okay, I'm not a writer; they are rejecting my articles." It never made a bit of difference to me. I didn't judge myself as a failure based on what other people think I should have done. It was just one more opportunity to learn and to prove that I could do something. When I give a speech, I must first please myself. I believe in what I do, and I get my satisfaction from completing it.

PSP: So, you don't care about whether people will buy?

Dr. Dyer: It's the work itself; it's what I do that counts. If they buy, it's just a bonus. It's advancing confidently in the direction of your own dream.

PSP: *Do you care about the positive reactions?*

Dr. Dyer: I love to hear positive reactions from people. I like getting good book sales. These are all wonderful things. I want them, but I don't need them. Ironically, you will meet with success in selling if you don't need to make the sale. That's the key. So, if I don't sell one book, I'm okay.

PSP: *That's a tough act to follow. If a salesperson doesn't make that big sale, he isn't likely to say, "I'm okay."*

Dr. Dyer: It's your choice. You don't need to interpret a lost sale as a rejection of yourself. If you need the sale to prove your self-worth, you will end up trying too hard. You'll be communicating that if you don't get it, you're going to be hurt, you're going to feel bad. So you'll come across as pushy; you'll be tempted to use guilt. All this comes from needing the sale. But you've got the choice to turn this around by conveying to that person, "If I make the sale, that's terrific; if I don't make the sale, that's fine too. I like you, and maybe we'll do business some other time."

PSP: *It sounds as if you don't believe that striving for the number one spot in your field is a good idea.*

Dr. Dyer: I think that is a very unhealthy, sick kind of concept.

PSP: *One of the most successful films in the field of sales motivation, entitled "Second Effort," has sold nearly 10,000 copies in the past ten years. The basic message is Vince Lombardi's famous quote, "Winning is the only thing."*

Dr. Dyer: I disagree vehemently.

PSP: *Why?*

Dr. Dyer: First of all, you cannot win all the time. Lombardi knew that. He was a great motivator, not because of his emphasis on winning but because he knew how to appeal to each one of his players on an individual, personal basis. Lombardi himself did not win all the time. He had to drink milk the last ten years of his life because of his ulcers; he was grossly overweight and died a very premature death. If you have to tell yourself that winning is the only thing, or if you define winning as having to beat somebody, you're going to be a loser. You can't win all the time. Ask Mohammed Ali, who was "the greatest"— sometimes!

PSP: *So, in selling, you could win more sales not by concentrating on winning but by . . .*

Dr. Dyer: When you depend on competition to win, you are putting somebody else in charge of your life. If you give up control over your emotional life, you're bound to suffer. When you're looking over your shoulder at the other guy and then deciding whether or not you are doing well based on comparing yourself with him, then he's in charge of your life. By looking over your shoulder, you'll end up losing; by looking inside, you'll find the keys to growth, self-improvement, and happiness.

PSP: *What exactly should you focus on when you look inside yourself?*

Dr. Dyer: In selling, your mental focus has to be on enjoying what you're doing, finding a sense of fulfillment.

PSP: *In your latest book,* Gifts from Eykis, *you write that it is preferable to stop listening to the outside world and to begin consulting your inner voices.*

Dr. Dyer: Right.

PSP: *Do you mean that most salespeople do not listen to their inner signals?*

Dr. Dyer: Most of us are trained not to trust what we're saying to ourselves.

PSP: *We are unaware of the importance of self-talk, and we're untrained in responding in self-enhancing ways.*

Dr. Dyer: Generally, we train people to trust somebody else.

PSP: How do you learn inner listening and inner responding?

Dr. Dyer: By practice; by doing it. There is no other way.

PSP: In your book, you're saying, "Your mind is the captain of the ship called your body." How do you propose that people get their captains' licenses?

Dr. Dyer: The only way to get that license is to begin practicing new things. You don't learn by someone else's telling you.

PSP: You make it sound so easy, as if you were saying the access to our subconscious mind is as easy as dialing a toll-free number.

Dr. Dyer: It's easier, because you don't need a telephone.

PSP: Let's say you're preparing for an important presentation. Before your big day, you wake up in the middle of the night because you've had a bad dream.

Dr. Dyer: You're the one who dreamed it; you take responsibility for your dreams. You can train yourself to dream or not to dream anything you want. We have all kinds of evidence to substantiate that. It's hard work to really get in tune with dreams, but I did that for one year. I recorded all my dreams. I forced myself to wake up every single night for a year just to find out what I was dreaming.

PSP: So you're saying that you can use your mind more efficiently by learning how to listen to its messages.

Dr. Dyer: When you set your mind to doing something, you can do anything. It can alter your heart rate; it can rid you of diseases. There is a will in everyone that is very difficult to describe. I see it when I run a marathon. I just ran a marathon yesterday—twenty-six point two miles. Since October 6, 1977, I have not missed one day of running a minimum of eight miles. Not one single day. There is a will in everyone that doesn't come from anything that is inherited or any electrochemical processes. It comes from the choices we make in our lives. Everything in life is a choice. I don't think it is a chemical imbalance that creates the way we think. I think it is the other way around; that is, our thinking indeed can create chemical imbalances. That's precisely what an ulcer is.

PSP: One of Zig Ziglar's concepts is "Garbage in—garbage out." You're saying that even if there is garbage around you, if you think happy thoughts, you could get chocolate cake out the other side?

Dr. Dyer: It may not necessarily be chocolate cake, but it's still a miracle; it's still something to appreciate. I've learned this from being around handicapped people, from having friends who are blind or deaf. People with handicaps often say, "I treat my handicap as a gift." It's not a curse; it's an opportunity. Look at some of the accounts from POWs. A POW is put in the worst conditions in the world, and the thing that saves him is his mind. His crucial choice is to think in a self-enhancing rather than a self-defeating manner.

PSP: I've heard comments from sales managers saying your books and tapes all sound very good. They like the promise of becoming self-actualized, but when they try to translate your ideas into everyday reality, they say it's easier said than done.

Dr. Dyer: We all keep falling down. And I do too. I fall down all the time, but I never said that no-limit people don't fall down. It's what you do when you fall down that makes you a no-limit person.

PSP: Could you give us an example of how you've fallen down and picked yourself up?

Dr. Dyer: You're talking to one of the biggest failures who ever lived. When *Erroneous Zones* came out and they told me there was no advertising budget, I said, "Well, then, I'll have to go out and do it myself." When they said that they couldn't distribute the book, I said, "I'll buy some; I'll take them with me." To me, that's an opportunity rather than an obstacle. If they don't have the money, then I'll have to take out a loan and do it myself. There was never a time when I said, "I guess I'll just have to give up on this." Successful people don't just land where they are on a parachute. You've got to climb up there; you've got to go through all the hurdles and look for the opportunities.

PSP: Let's assume that in spite of your efforts, your book didn't sell. You lost all your money. Would you have succeeded in thinking happy thoughts?

Dr. Dyer: Sure. No question. When I got down to writing it, I never thought I'd make a nickel on it. I had been writing for five years and never made any money.

PSP: Why did you write it?

Dr. Dyer: I wrote it for me. I felt that I had something to say that hadn't been said.

PSP: Aren't you in a way talking like someone who has $2 million in his bank account and says making money is easy?

Dr. Dyer: I was saying the same thing when I was working as a bag boy at a supermarket in Detroit, when I was shining shoes or driving a cab. I always had money. I grew up in an orphanage, and I know about things like hunger from experience. I've never had an allowance; I've never had anybody give me a nickel in my life. Still, people think I'm talking from the perspective of a rich guy. I've been alive forty-two and a half years, and I have been rich only a few of those. I always had more than one job, because I didn't care for unemployment benefits or blaming the economy. I knew I had to go out and get a job. Not only did I get one, I had one in the morning, one in the afternoon, and another at night, plus going to school on top of it.

PSP: What's your definition of success?

Dr. Dyer: Living your life the way you choose to, without interfering with anybody else's right to do the same.

PSP: In your book, The Sky's the Limit, *you've made the promise of becoming a no-limit person. What about delivery?*

Dr. Dyer: I deliver for myself, and that's all I can take responsibility for. I am an example of somebody who has come out of a family where nobody went to college. We were as poor as you can get. My parents got divorced when I was one year old; my stepfather was an abusive alcoholic. I'm saying that you don't have to use your childhood as an excuse for not growing. It is never too late to have a happy childhood. I've a sign on my mirror that says, "Maybe we can change the world if we start with ourselves." It was sent to me by somebody who read one of my books. I look at it every day and I say, "Just take responsibility for yourself. Do what you can."

PSP: You seem to be very firm in separating your responsibility and that of others. When I did the research for this interview, I got this comment from a well-known psychiatrist and author who listened to one of your tapes: "He shows little empathy and appears somewhat narcissistic." Do you feel that's true?

Dr. Dyer: I know that's a notion a lot of people have. I am aware that your reputation is totally outside your control, only your character is made by yourself. Everybody who knows me knows that for every dollar that I spend on myself, I spend ten on other people. I always have been generous to a fault. There are a lot of things that I do because I feel they are helpful to other people. I see myself as a giver. I give a lot of money to charity. I spend a lot of my time to help unfortunate people. Yet, this still comes from *enjoying* what I do for others. I am not an "I–I–I, me–me–me" person. I know, if you listen to some of my tapes, they do in fact give that impression. I admit that. It's something I have tried to correct. In fact, my new book *Eykis* will dispel a lot of that, because Eykis is love. I think I have grown.

DR. WAYNE DYER: KEY IDEAS TO REMEMBER

1. If you give up control over your emotional life, you're bound to suffer. By looking inside, you'll find the keys to growth, self-improvement, and happiness.

2. Solution-oriented thinking comes from sharing and loving. You should be so involved in helping another human being that your own needs become un-important.

3. You will meet with success in selling if you don't need to make the sale. If you need to make the sale to prove your self-worth, you will end up trying too hard.

4. Communicate to other people (prospects) that you really care about them as people rather than as buyers of your product.

5. If you're a person who really, truly believes in yourself and the possibility of reaching your dreams, then that will come through and other people will want more of you.

Now please complete the Action Plan on the following page.

MY ACTION PLAN FOR SUCCESS

1.

2.

3.

4.

5.

5

Portrait of Motivation:

ZIG ZIGLAR

It is easy to be motivated by Zig Ziglar. His tone of voice alone communicates the message that attitude is the key to success in life. His whole being is a study of motivation in action.

When I watched him during a Personal Development Day rally organized by his nephew, John Ziglar, I found myself being swept along on the wave of optimism and certainty that he creates.

I felt ready for anything, a feeling often shared by those who listen to him. But what struck me more than the surge in adrenalin was how much I carried away after the meeting and how long it stayed with me. To this day I find myself quoting his punchlines, aphorisms, or "mental snacks" that express a profound but often overlooked truth governing our daily lives.

During our long and extensive interview, I realized that Zig Ziglar is more than simply a motivator. He is a person with a strong, well-established guiding philosophy, one that has something of enduring value for everyone. He expresses it with the words, "You can get everything in life you want, if you help enough other people get what they want."

This maxim is certainly true in selling, but it is equally true in any other field. By helping others, you help yourself. We live in a world of interdependence and mutuality.

During my research, I've talked to several people who dismissed Zig's motivational meetings as hot air designed to pump them up without achieving a significant change in attitude.

Nearly all of the critics seemed to carry poorly defined notions of the subject of self-motivation. "You can't graduate in self-motivation," explained Zig in our interview after a long reflective pause. His answer made me realize that it is not his responsibility to change other people's attitudes. He can only present the tools; it's up to his audience to use them. Motivation for Zig is a daily necessity like eating and bathing.

It has been more than a year since I interviewed him, and his guiding philosophy of helping others is still serving me every day.

If one is to learn from Zig about becoming a Superachiever, one must listen to him intently and then put into practice what he presents. Knowledge increases with repeated practice. Many people have turned their lives around because they decided to apply Zig's principles to improve their lives.

An impeccable person to deal with, Zig Ziglar's foundation reflects integrity and inner strength. He is convinced that we have a profound effect on one another and that it is important to make positive contacts to get positive results.

The age-old question of whether the glass is half full or half empty is still with us. The only change is that today we are lucky enough to have Zig Ziglar to help us see the glass waiting to be filled to the brim, by us. If you follow Zig's guiding philosophy, your glass will never again be half empty.

AMERICA'S NUMBER ONE MOTIVATOR

Are you one of the people who pooh-poohs positive thinking as a tool used only by the meek and weak? Read on! Zig Ziglar is out to change your thoughts, your attitude, and perhaps, your life.

On the slick red, white, and blue dust jacket of his book See You at the Top *(with sales approaching one million copies), he promises a "checkup" from the "neck up" to eliminate "stinkin' thinkin'."*

Ziglar's electrifying speeches have a reputation for drawing long standing ovations and leaving audiences spellbound. Trailing a microphone wire behind him, Zig speeds across the stage in Norfolk, Virginia. He has the eyes of 2000 salespeople following his every move. His rate of speech bursts up to 500 words per minute. He squats and slowly raises his left hand. His voice begins to vibrate as it approaches a near stall. He relishes every single word of his famous punchline: "You can get everything in life you want, if you help enough other people get what they want."

Ziglar is his own best success story. It began in Yazoo City, Mississippi. He was born one of twelve children. His father died when he was five, leaving his mother with five kids too young to work.

He became one of the most successful cookware salesmen of all time but quit knocking on doors when he recognized his charisma for motivating others.

Although Zig has been interviewed by many reporters (including Morley Safer of "60 Minutes"), Personal Selling Power *felt a need to explore new answers to the familiar question facing salespeople in today's economy: "What can I do to motivate myself?"*

PSP: In one of your speeches you mentioned that negative thinking is as common as the cold. Did you find a cure for negative thinking?

Ziglar: If you feed your mind with positive thoughts, if you are selective about the things that you choose to read, look at, or listen to, then you are taking effective action against negative thinking. It's just like with a computer; if you change the input, you will change the output.

PSP: So you are saying that there is a direct link between negative thinking and negative input and that people can become more selective about the input?

Ziglar: Absolutely. Let me give you an example. Thomas M. Hartman from Oklahoma City weighed 407 pounds when he attended a rally in January 1978. He had just gone through a devastating divorce; he was floating checks so he could eat from one week to the next; he held a job only because his boss was a friend, not because he was productive. During our all-day seminar he began to think that he could do something. He got a set of my tapes, *How to Stay Motivated,* and started listening. He told me he has heard that set more than 500 times. He could quote me verbatim from start to finish. Today, Tom weighs 200 pounds; he's happily remarried; he teaches a Sunday school class every week. He graduated *magna cum laude* in psychology and is working toward his doctorate. He's in business for himself.

PSP: *It sounds like your positive input has helped him to lead a more successful life. What is your definition of success?*

Ziglar: I believe that you're successful when you've dealt with the physical, the mental, and the spiritual man successfully. If I made millions and destroyed my health in the process, or if I become the best at what I do but neglect my family, I wouldn't call that success.

PSP: *One of your claims is that your attitudes in life determine ultimately how successful you become.*

Ziglar: Yes. Dr. William James said the most important discovery of our time is the realization that by altering our attitudes we can alter our lives. There is also a Harvard University study that points out that 85 percent of the reason people are hired or get ahead in their jobs is directly related to their attitudes.

PSP: *A magazine entitled* California Living *recently stated in an article about motivational speakers, "Speakers are superficial on the subject of motivation—like cheerleaders at a high school rally. Thin on content; heavy on performance." How do you respond to that?*

Ziglar: I think they are right on the button. A lot of people do leave without any real meat. Excitement, yes, but nothing they can chew on the next day.

As you know, the Bible is my great source, because

God's plan deals with this dilemma: He never makes a promise unless he gives you a plan. This translates into the principle that motivation without direction is very frustrating. You need to have a plan in addition to the motivation. Motivation without a goal doesn't get you anywhere. Personally, I never make a promise in a book, a speech, or a recording unless I give a plan so my reader or listener can achieve the promise.

PSP: What is your theory of self-motivation? How do you develop it?

Ziglar: From time to time, in some egghead discussions with my intellectual friends, I'm told that all motivation is self-motivation. I respond to that in *See You at the Top* with a little analogy. When I build a fire in my fireplace, it will burn for a while. Then I notice that there are no flames. It has died down. I get up and take my poker and shake up those logs. All of a sudden, we've got bright flames. Now, all I did was just poke them, which created some motion. The motion creates a partial vacuum and new air is pulled into the fireplace. With an additional supply of oxygen, the fire ignites, and now we've got a flame. If I hadn't done some poking, there would have been no flame.

Now, this business about all motivation being self-motivation is only partially true. You can choose among many different sources to rekindle your motivation. In other words, the environment you select and the people you associate with become large contributing factors.

PSP: Positive relationships will contribute to positive motivation?

Ziglar: Certainly. One day I heard my son saying, "The thing I like best about my Dad is that he loves Mom." You see, positive relationships create a feeling of closeness and become a source of strength. The likelihood of motivating yourself is greatly increased with positive relationships.

The equation also works the other way. I've been active in the war against drugs for a long time. I strongly believe that a person is inclined to use dope in direct proportion to the number of times it is offered to him.

PSP: And to the frustrations that he is carrying around without knowing how to deal with them.

Ziglar: Yes, he might say no seventeen times, but then that one day comes when he's had a bad day and feels frustrated and exasperated, and is unable to recognize the danger and is bound to suffer in the long run.

PSP: Do you feel that the exclusive focus on the positive side of life can lead to a new set of problems?

Ziglar: There is always a possibility. I do believe, though, that if you were to take a hundred cases, you'd find ninety-five times that the positive response is going to be the right approach.

PSP: You are familiar with Sam Cooper. He attended one of your seminars in 1976. According to a magazine report, he was moved as never before about his own potential for greatness. Two years later he was a millionaire. By 1979, Esquire *magazine reports, he grossed more than $10 million in the motivational seminar business. But in 1980, the* Memphis Call Bulletin *described Cooper's massive financial setbacks and his failure to fulfill his commitments to hundreds of subscribers to his* Positive Living Magazine. *Isn't that an example of how excessive optimism can lead to an unrealistic appraisal of one's true abilities?*

Ziglar: Well, there is no question about it in that case. First of all, Sam Cooper did not use sound business judgment, and every time you violate that law you're ultimately going to end up in trouble.

PSP: So, in other words, the positive input and the positive attitude need to be supplemented with a sound business plan and professional skills.

Ziglar: Absolutely. Let me sum it up this way. Positive thinking is an optimistic hope, not necessarily based on any facts. Positive believing is the same optimistic hope, but this time based on a sound reason. Here is an example. It would be positive thinking if I said I could whip Larry Holmes. It would be an idiotic action if I tried to do it.

PSP: I've heard many sales managers express doubts about the value of a motivational seminar. They say, "Our people get fired up for a while and they are totally enthusiastic, but two days later they're back in the same old groove—nothing changed."

Ziglar: Well, let me refer to it indirectly. Another reporter once asked in a different way the same question. He said, "The charge is that motivation is not permanent. How do you respond to that?" And I said, "Absolutely right!" It is not permanent. Neither is bathing. But if you bathe every day, you're going to smell good. In my seminars I explain that fifteen minutes a day of motivation from a good audio cassette or a book can make a tremendous difference in your life and give you a motivational lift *every* day.

PSP: You've said once that life is simple but not easy, and that too many people are looking for quick and easy solutions.

Ziglar: Right.

PSP: The answers that you give in your speeches and your cassette tapes, are they simple and easy to apply?

Ziglar: Simple and easy to understand. But I'll never tell you life is easy. There are a lot of days when you don't feel like doing your job. But I firmly believe that the best work is often done by people who don't feel like doing it. You know, the mother wakes up at two o'clock a.m. with her baby crying; she's had a tough night and a tough day, but she's gonna get up because of love and responsibility.

PSP: You recommend that salespeople should listen to your tapes sixteen times to completely absorb the full message?

Ziglar: Let me explain why I suggest they listen so many times. There are several university studies revealing that two weeks after you've learned anything new, unless it's reinforced, you only remember about 4 percent of it. That's the first reason. The second reason is that while we are listening we may experience a certain mood, and our minds will seek out messages that relate to that particular mood. On another day, let's say you just made a sale; you'll be in a different mood, and a whole new range of messages of the same recording will become clear in your mind. So by listening sixteen times, the odds are that you will have absorbed the entire content.

PSP: Let's say I've listened sixteen times to your tapes on motivation. Do I know then how to motivate myself?

Ziglar: Yes.

PSP: Do I master the skills sufficiently so that I become independent of your cassette?

Ziglar: Only if you've been practicing the things we've been advocating. It's like driving a car. You don't learn to drive a car by watching.

PSP: Can I graduate in self-motivation, ever?

Ziglar: Boy, that's a tough one. Nobody has ever asked me that before. I don't think so, and I don't think I've graduated, because I constantly read and constantly study. I think you could draw an analogy with eating. You can't graduate in eating. You need to continue to make choices about your input. The same is true with self-motivation. You need to continue to make choices about what level of self-motivation you want to maintain.

PSP: You seem to have an unusual ability to create persuasive analogies to illustrate your point. In your book, See You at the Top, *you've used more than 800 analogies, one-liners, and power phrases. How did you develop this technique?*

Ziglar: Well, one of the things I did when I first got interested in motivation was to buy a yearly datebook, and on the top of every page there was a power phrase, a one-liner. So I started writing them down. This was long before the days of cassette recordings. I wrote them on three-by-five cards and I put them up on the visor of my car. And I'd be riding down the highway and think about them. Over the years, I committed to memory several hundred of them.

PSP: Many salespeople have a tough time in this economy. What thoughts can you offer to approach these tough challenges more positively?

Ziglar: A good friend of mine, Calvin Hunt in Victoria, Texas, said, "You know, Zig, it's an absolute fact that when we are in an economic slump, 50 percent of all salespeople literally slow down rather than speed up their efforts. They are not motivated to do something. They lose that enthusiasm.

"Now," he continued, "when that happens, it simply means that if business is down 20 percent, but 50 percent of the salespeople are not nearly as active, your own personal prospect list is considerably higher than if there was no recession."

PSP: And the winners still keep winning.

Ziglar: Absolutely. It's their discipline, their commitment to maintain a high level of motivation, and their sense of direction that gets them to the top.

ZIG'S KEY TO SALES SUCCESS

Zig Ziglar offers many excellent selling tips in his seminars:

- Have an absolute and total belief that what you're selling is worth more than the price you ask for it. Your belief in your product should be so great that you ought to be using it.
- Mentally prepare yourself. Review your product knowledge and selling skills before every call. Try to write down your presentation, and you'll discover that you are using too many words, that you drift away from the point, or that you are not specific enough. Writing will remind you of something you've forgotten and help you generate better selling ideas.

- Use emotion *and* logic in your presentation. Logic makes people think; emotion makes them act. For example, in selling cookware, we would take the logical approach and explain that, according to USDA, the average shrinkage of a four-pound roast in the oven or in the ordinary pot was one pound seven ounces. Cooking it in our method, you lost five ounces. Logically, you could say, "If you had a cook that stole one pound of your roast every time he cooked one, you'd fire him. No hesitation! Here, you've got this old, beat-up pot that's been stealing from you for twenty years. I think it's time you fired it. Fire that old pot and get a new one. And it's not going to steal from you!" That would make sense logically.

- Then, we would say from a practical point of view, we are what we eat. If the food you put in your body is short on nutrition, then eventually you are going to pay for it. Sometimes I'd say, "Our set of cookware will help your baby grow up with a better chance at good health."

- We combined the logic on the dollar and the emotion on the good health for better results. You need to balance these keys. If you use all logic, you end up with the best-educated prospect in town. If you use all emotion, you make the sale, but tomorrow you'll have the buyer's remorse and a canceled order.

ZIG'S FIRST SALE

It was on a hot August afternoon in 1947. It happened on Adelia Drive in Columbia, South Carolina. I'd been knocking on doors all afternoon, and nobody would let me in. I made a solemn vow that if I didn't at least get into a house by the time I got to Devine Street, I was going to quit. I'd been working ten days and had not sold anything.

I knocked on the door of Mrs. B. C. Dickert, and she said, "Well, you know, it sounds interesting, but my sister-in-law, Mrs. J. O. Freeman, lives next door, and I know she'd be interested. Why don't you go talk to her, and if she looks at it, just call me over."

So, I literally ran next door—that was the first word of

encouragement I'd heard all day—and I talked to Mrs. Freeman. She said, "Well, I'd want my husband to see it."

So, I said, "Well, I'll come back tonight." So, I got back that night, and they invited Mrs. Dickert over. I finished the presentation and I can tell you that it was set number 541, that it cost $61.45, that the down payment was $16.45, and that when I sold the Freemans I was so enamoured and excited that I just flat forgot that Mrs. Dickert even lived. I just ignored her. And finally, Mr. Freeman said, "Mr. Ziglar, I believe that if you were to talk to Mrs. Dickert, she might buy a set."

And so, with considerable sales technique and skill, I said, "What about it, Mrs. Dickert?"

She said, "Well, I don't have my checkbook, even."

And again, with considerable diplomacy, I said, "Well, shoot, you just live next door. Go get it!" And she went next door, so I made two sales that night.

We lived in a little upstairs apartment, and I didn't hit more than two steps on the way up that night. That redhead knew that something had happened. I tell you, we were just elated! We jumped up and down and laughed and celebrated by buying two quarts of ice cream.

ZIG ZIGLAR: KEY IDEAS TO REMEMBER

1. We can't graduate in self-motivation. It's like eating. We can't graduate in eating. We need to continue to make choices about what level of self-motivation we want to maintain.

2. The likelihood of motivating yourself is greatly increased with positive relationships. Positive relationships create a feeling of closeness and become a source of strength.

3. If you feed your mind with positive thoughts, if you are selective about the things that you choose to read, look at, or listen to, then you are taking effective action against negative thinking.

4. Success is not measured by what you've done compared to others but compared to what you're capable of doing.

5. To succeed in selling, use emotion and logic in your sales presentation. Logic makes people think; emotion makes them act. If you use only logic, you'll end up with the best-educated prospect in town. If you use only emotion, you'll end up with a canceled order. Balance these keys and you'll sell more.

Now please complete the Action Plan on the following page.

MY ACTION PLAN FOR SUCCESS

1.

2.

3.

4.

5.

6

Portrait of Mental Health:

DR. DAVID BURNS

Do you remember philosopher William James's famous statement, "What the mind can conceive and believe, it can achieve"?

Most people who read this quote interpret it to mean that we all have the ability to consciously develop, imagine, and believe in positive thoughts and to turn these thoughts into reality.

In other words, if you conceive the thought of becoming the president of your company, and if you put the proper amount of belief into this thought, you'll end up achieving your career goal.

William James's quote appears to be working as long as we assume that we possess the magic power of keeping our minds focused long enough on positive thoughts and as long as we assume that our belief systems are totally immune to changes, revisions, conflicts, or simple lapses of memory.

I am not saying that William James is wrong. On the contrary, his statement has as much validity today as on the day he wrote it. However, only very few people realize that "what the mind can conceive and believe, it can achieve" applies equally well to negative thoughts.

We all know that our ability to conceive negative thoughts is so great that we can end up believing them. We can indeed turn negative thoughts into reality with the result that we feel miserable. These negative thoughts and feelings will last until we find our way out of the mental maze.

As much as we would like to keep our minds focused on positive thoughts, the fact is that we simply cannot prevent our minds from producing negative thoughts. (Read also

Dr. Norman Vincent Peale's comment on this subject in Chapter 13.)

The two questions left unanswered by William James are:

1. How can we consciously dissolve negative thoughts?
2. How can we pinpoint, examine, and manage negative thoughts as soon as they are conceived?

It took a Superachiever of the mind, Dr. David Burns, to convince me that our ability to deal with negative thoughts holds another important key to achievement and success.

Dr. Burns is the Director of the Institute for Cognitive and Behavioral Therapies at the Presbyterian-University of Pennsylvania Medical Center, a best-selling author, and an international lecturer.

I remember the day I first saw his book, *Feeling Good: The New Mood Therapy,* in a bookstore. As I opened the book, I read the sentence that said, "Twisted thinking is the exclusive cause of nearly all your suffering." The day after I bought the book, I found a small package in the mail from Suzy Sutton, *Personal Selling Power*'s contributing editor. She had sent an audio recording of an interview she had conducted with Dr. David Burns for a radio station in Philadelphia. She mentioned in a note that the interview resulted in a flood of phone calls.

I immediately listened to their conversation and found it so fascinating that I decided to test Dr. Burns's new thought management method to dissolve my own negative thoughts. I could hardly wait for the appearance of negative thoughts in my mind. I waited. Several days later, I found myself in a ridiculously stupid, self-denigrating internal dialogue about a supplier's mistake in the production of an important advertising brochure. I was so involved in blaming myself and feeling frustrated that I completely forgot to try the new techniques. As I kept mumbling, my secretary, who had glanced through the book, suggested putting *Feeling Good* to the test.

I immediately went through the double-column technique, and, to my surprise, I was able to flush the negative thoughts from my mind. In less than ten minutes I began to feel quite pleased with myself. I realized that the method for managing negative thoughts had actually saved an unpleasant hour of stewing, brooding, and feeling bad.

I obtained permission to edit and print Suzy's interview. Dr. Burns graciously offered to expand and adapt the material for our readers, and he has since repeatedly shared his expertise for the benefit of all who read *Personal Selling Power*. I feel privileged every time we talk, because he has helped me realize that all the success in the world can lose its meaning if you don't know how to feel good.

Dr. Burns demonstrates in thought and action that the greatest success in the world is self-esteem, along with a positive regard for others.

GETTING HOOKED ON FEELING GOOD

PSP: Many sales executives feel the economic crunch. I spoke last week to a group of sixty sales executives, and they appeared very negative; some were angry or depressed. Now you've written a book that has recently entered the best-seller lists, called Feeling Good. *What kind of techniques could some of these salespeople use to take them out of their negative feelings?*

Dr. Burns: Well, first of all, we have to understand why people feel negative, angry, or depressed, as in the situation you've described. My book describes a new theory called cognitive theory. Essentially, it means that your moods are created by your thoughts. Other theories assume that your thoughts are caused by forces beyond your control, such as external events, your body chemistry, or your subconcious mind, but what we are learning is that your moods are, to a great extent, caused by forces within your control, the way you're thinking about things.

PSP: You mean "cognitive" means self-created? In other words, these sales executives created their own negative moods through negative thoughts?

Dr. Burns: Yes, cognitive means the way you are thinking at any given point. To give you a simple example, I think, just a moment ago, I used the wrong word in a sentence. So I might then have the thought, "My gosh, I am goofing up, I am doing terribly." That thought, if I believe it, would create a certain emotional response, namely anxiety or depression or a sense of defeat. When people are upset, or depressed, they are virtually always thinking in a negative manner. But what's more interesting, these negative thoughts are frequently twisted, illogical, or distorted. What they are telling themselves is often not an accurate reflection of reality. Now, the real scientific breakthrough is that by training individuals to think about things in a more realistic way, and to talk back to those negative thoughts, you can often see very positive changes in mood.

PSP: In other words, all the proponents and all the preachers who have been proposing the fact that a positive mental attitude affects your body and your mind in a positive way, all that has been and is true?

Dr. Burns: Yes, I hate to admit it, but the academic world is now beginning to agree with what some of the philosophers of the lay public have been saying for many years, namely that your thoughts and outlook and sense of trust in yourself affect your moods. If you are thinking about things in a defeatist and negative way, you are going to experience anger and depression.

PSP: I can hear all those sales executives out there saying, "Well, that's well and good, but how do we chase these negative thoughts from our minds? How do you replace the negativity with positive thinking?"

Dr. Burns: This is where the new mood therapy has a great deal to offer. We've developed a lot of techniques that can help people overcome patterns of negative thinking and boost their productivity and self-esteem.

PSP: Have you ever worked with sales groups?

Dr. Burns: Certainly. I've worked with individual sales representatives here in my practice. I'm also involved in ongoing studies, where we measure their attitudes toward themselves and compare how these attitudes influence their sales performances.

PSP: Could we talk about how your technique would work with an individual salesperson and then discuss your research with groups?

Dr. Burns: Yes. I remember a salesman who came to see me not too long ago. He was good-looking, intelligent, and very personable. His problem was fairly common: the fear of calling on new prospects.

PSP: How could you help him?

Dr. Burns: Simply by exploring his negative thoughts. For example, he would say to himself, "What if the customer gets turned off and thinks I'm a jerk?" or, "I am afraid of feeling rejected!" Now, the technique consists of talking back to your thoughts. How would you talk back to these negative thoughts?

PSP: Well, if I were the salesman, I would say, "Some people will buy my product, and others will turn me down. I'm a human being and not a jerk."

Dr. Burns: Good.

PSP: And I do the best I can.

Dr. Burns: Good, and your rational response to the second thought, to "I am afraid of being rejected," would be what?

PSP: Well, I guess I would say, "If I don't take chances, I don't get anywhere!"

Dr. Burns: How about more zeroing in on the fear of rejection? Is it really the salesperson that the customer rejects?

PSP: Oh, I understand. So I could talk back and say, "I am not being rejected, only my sales proposal."
Dr. Burns: That's right.

PSP: In other words, what you are explaining with your method is that we have a choice to feel good and we have a choice to feel bad.
Dr. Burns: That's right, and the new mood therapy involves a hundred ways to make this choice more accessible to salespeople and people from all walks of life.

PSP: How about your research with groups where you measured their attitudes toward themselves?
Dr. Burns: For example, I studied a group of insurance salespeople from the Philadelphia Million Dollar Forum. I predicted that the perfectionists would be more stressed but more successful. I was surprised that there was absolutely no evidence for this. In fact, many of the perfectionists were actually earning less than their more relaxed colleagues.

PSP: These people produced less because they believed they had to be perfect?
Dr. Burns: Yes. Many salespeople don't realize that they are subscribing to a self-defeating belief system that says, "To be worthwhile, I must achieve." This attitude is not helping them at all, because when they fail to achieve a goal, they feel they have failed as human beings. This creates a tremendous sense of pressure to succeed, which can actually reduce your effectiveness; it makes you vulnerable to bouts of depression and anxiety. Depression is the world's greatest enemy of creativity and productivity.

PSP: Now, if a sales manager could help these people to change their attitudes, would they be able to increase their sales?
Dr. Burns: I would not be able to give you an exact percentage, but I believe that their sales would go up by some amount. I'm now analyzing data on over 1,000 individuals from around the United States to see how perfectionism affects career satisfaction and performance. Hope-

fully, this will shed more light on the crucial but subtle difference between compulsive perfectionism and the healthy pursuit of excellence.

PSP: How do you define self-esteem?

Dr. Burns: Well, let me start with the word *self-confidence,* since many people have problems in separating these terms. Self-confidence is the idea that you'll be successful at something because you've been successful in the past. Like you; you are self-confident about conducting interviews, because you've done it many times before and you're well received. I define self-esteem as the ability to love or like yourself whether or not you are successful. Self-love is self-esteem. It does not have to be earned. It can't be earned through love, through achievement, through perfection. You can give it to yourself without having to prove anything.

PSP: So you are suggesting that salespeople should not connect their performance to their self-esteem. But isn't this counterproductive? Most of their egos depend on being a winner, being number one, being the best. How can you avoid saying, "To be worthwhile I must achieve," or "I can't be happy unless I'm number one"?

Dr. Burns: These belief systems are fooling them, but they think that they are helping them. They are unaware of their choice. You can either love yourself on the basis of your strengths or your weaknesses. To me, self-love is what you need when you're suffering. Think of it in another way. Why do you hug a child? Because the child is crying and needs your love. Would you say that your children have to go out and run a race and get a blue ribbon before you'll give them love? Why do you give your children love? I give my children love when they need it most, when they are afraid, when they are frightened, when they are failing to reach a goal. If I would say that you have to link your self-esteem to your performance as a salesperson, I'd suggest that you give yourself the greatest amount of love and support when you fall short of a goal and you feel discouraged.

Anyone can feel good about themselves when they succeed, but the secret of real self esteem is the ability to love and support yourself when you fail. I give myself love unconditionally, because I am a human being and I don't have to earn it through work, through being perfect, through being loved, or through being approved of by others. I just declare it. I love myself because that's my decision. Because I want to feel good!

PSP: So, in other words, self-esteem is an emotion of how warm and loving you feel toward yourself, no matter what happens outside you?

Dr. Burns: Exactly. And if you can be more warm and loving in the face of failure and rejection—for example, when you've lost that important sale—then you have real self-esteem. If you can only be warm and loving if others love you first, or when they approve of you, or when you are a big success, that's pseudo-esteem.

PSP: That's what I call canned confidence.

Dr. Burns: We are on the same wavelength.

PSP: I've conducted seminars on self-esteem and know how important it is to develop healthy self-esteem. But your new book seems to deal more with ways to handle clinical depression.

Dr. Burns: Yes, but also the areas of low self-esteem that people feel in their everyday life. Like your group of salespeople you mentioned earlier. The methods can be used to tune up a life that has not been riddled by severe depression.

PSP: How do you tell that you are depressed?

Dr. Burns: Well, if you're depressed, you feel down in the dumps, blue, sad. Life has lost its vitality. You might feel irritable. You may lose your interests, you feel blah . . .

PSP: But doesn't everyone feel like that once in a while, maybe for a day or two?

Dr. Burns: I think virtually everybody does. It's really as common as the cold. But the difference is, you can't do anything about the cold, but there is something that can be done about depression. You can do something to snap out of it, fight back.

PSP: The main method is, of course, taking control of your own mind and changing the negative thinking into positive thinking. But what motivates you to do this? What steps can you take to actually do this?

Dr. Burns: It depends on the kind of problem the person has. The book I've written shows if someone fears disapproval, how to learn to get over that; if someone fears criticism, how to handle that; if someone is unmotivated, or lying in bed, how they can get themselves motivated. For example, let's say an individual fears being unloved and has a belief system saying, "My worth as a human being depends on being loved and, if I am unloved, I can't be happy." Well, I might ask the individual to make a list of the advantages and disadvantages of believing that assumption. So he or she might say, "Well, the advantage of that is while I am loved, I feel terrific. The disadvantage is on those many occasions when I don't get as much love as I want, I go into a depression. Or people can manipulate me, because they know if I am unloved I'll get depressed, so they can force me into doing whatever they want." I might have the client develop a list so he or she can appraise his or her belief system more objectively. Then I might suggest many ways that could prove that it was not even true in the first place.

PSP: I see, what you're saying is that when you are dealing with reality—with what is happening, not with what you think is happening—depression will fly out the window?

Dr. Burns: That's exactly right. We've seen that when people are depressed, they are always engaging in twisted thinking. There are ten forms of twisted thinking described in my book. We've seen that whenever a person is depressed, he or she is twisting reality in one or more of these ten ways.

PSP: That sounds like a self-fulfilling prophecy.

They want to feel bad, so they make things conform to their thoughts.

Dr. Burns: No, we don't think it's wanting to feel bad. We think it's habit. They don't realize their habitual patterns of distortion. For example, one form of twisted thinking is overgeneralization. Let's say a sales rep saw a customer who rejected his or her proposal. He or she might leave the customer's office saying, "Oh, my gosh, it's all over for me. I don't have what it takes to be a good sales rep. I am a real failure and a loser and I might as well give up." That would be overgeneralization.

PSP: *What do your peers think of this new technique of talking back to your negative and unrealistic thoughts?*

Dr. Burns: Well, when this approach began to gain recognition in the early to mid-1970s, there was a lot of skepticism. I myself felt very skeptical because it seemed too simple.

Then many research studies began to show that it was actually as effective as drugs in the treatment of severely depressed individuals. So psychiatrists and psychologists began to pay attention to what we were saying; they could no longer discount it. There have now been many studies around the world which confirm the effectiveness of this approach. In fact, the National Institute of Mental Health has recently initiated a $3.4 million multi-university study to investigate this new approach. This will compare its effectiveness to drug therapy and to a more traditional form of psychotherapy at six universities. This is one of the largest psychotherapy studies in history.

PSP: *Could your book actually help someone to get out of negative feelings or depression alone, without going to your Mood Clinic?*

Dr. Burns: I've had letters from people from all over the country who have written and said, "I've been depressed for a number of years, I've read your book, and I thank you that I finally found happiness." I recently received, around the holidays, a moving letter from a reader who wrote: "God bless you for giving me my first happy Christmas in as long as I can remember." Now, whether these good feelings will stick, I don't know. I like to teach people not only to feel good but also to reapply the techniques, so they can continue to master the bad moods that come up from time to time. That can require an ongoing effort.

PSP: Your book, Feeling Good, *shows how to build the sound self-esteem necessary to feel good. This is something every salesperson could use. Because when you have good self-esteem, then all this anger, the emotional upsets, and the depression go out the window.*

Dr. Burns: That's right. I don't think you can be depressed and have good self-esteem. I think self-esteem is the enemy of depression and most emotional upsets in this world. That's the bottom line.

CHANGING SELF-DEFEATING BELIEFS OF SUCCESS

For example, a life insurance sales rep's belief system says, "My worth as a human being depends on selling $6 million of life insurance this year. If I don't sell that much, I can't feel happy and worthwhile."

To help appraise this erroneous belief system, the sales rep could consider appraising the advantages and disadvantages of his beliefs as in the example illustrated below.

Advantages

"This belief system keeps me motivated, it helps me make more calls, it helps me reach my goals, it helps me make money, and it gives me a purpose in life."

Disadvantages

"When I don't reach my goal, I get angry, upset, or depressed. This belief system also brings a great deal of doubt and worry about my capabilities. This belief system makes me ignore my needs for feeling good. This belief system makes me angry and upset each time I lose a sale; this

(*continued on p. 90*)

4 STEP PROCESS OF FEELING BAD

3 ROADBLOCKS PREVENTING CHANGE

1. EXPERIENCE

For example, a sales manager tells one of her best sales reps, "Jack, normally we would invite you to fly to our main office for the annual executive dinner, but for budget reasons we can't do that. This year we have invited only our top executives."

1. UNAWARE OF SELF-TALK

Chances are that Jack is not aware of how his brief experience was translated into a series of twisted and distorted thoughts. It was not the manager who created the negative feelings; it was Jack's distorted thinking that led to the negative feelings.

2. DISTORTED SELF-TALK

As Jack's experience is filtered through his erroneous belief system, he may develop distorted thoughts, such as, "I am just not good enough, I am just second rate . . . I should have gone to college . . . they don't value my work . . . I hate these executive dinners anyway . . . The hell with it all!"

2. UNAWARE OF BELIEF SYSTEM

Jack may not have been aware of how much he needed to be recognized and approved of by others. He doesn't know that his self-esteem depends on being perceived as one of the top producers by the company's top management. Even if he is aware of the belief system, he is unaware that it is hurtful and self-defeating.

3. BELIEF SYSTEM

Jack's erroneous belief system states, "My worth as a human being depends on receiving everybody's recognition. I must be among the top, or I am no good at all."

4. NEGATIVE FEELINGS

"I am just not good enough.
I am just second rate"........ *depression/ inferiority*

"I should have gone to college" ...*guilt*

"They don't value my work" .... *resentment*

"I hate these executive dinners anyway"........................... *anger*

"The hell with it all!"......... *frustration*

3. UNAWARE OF SELF-MANAGEMENT TECHNIQUE

Jack does not know how to deal with his negative feelings. His negative self-talk will continue, and the feelings of anger, frustration, and depression will persist for some time. Jack's mind is like a blackboard that has not been erased. He's stuck in a negative point of view and dwells on his imagined inadequacy. Jack is puzzled by the fact that he can't see the problem objectively. The negative feelings can negatively influence his performance as well as his life and career satisfaction.

2 STEP METHOD FOR FEELING GOOD

1. WRITE YOUR SELF-TALK ON PAPER

Start managing your thoughts by dividing the paper with one vertical line. List your automatic thoughts on the left-hand side.

Jack could have used this method by writing on the left-hand side:

Self-Talk	Objective Appraisal
I am just not good enough. I am just second rate. I should have gone to college. They don't value my work. I hate these executive dinners anyway. The hell with it all.	

2. APPRAISE YOUR SELF-TALK

After you've completed your list of automatic thoughts, start with appraising each thought in a realistic and objective way.

Jack could have appraised his thoughts by writing on the right hand side:

Self-Talk	Objective Appraisal
I am just not good enough. I am just second rate.	Not true. I am a top sales rep. My performance this year has been excellent. I can't write myself off because there has been a budget problem.
I should have gone to college.	I decided to go into sales. That was my choice, and I like my job.
They don't value my work.	This is not true. I've earned more than $12,000 in commission on top of my salary this year. This is good compensation for my work.
I hate these executive dinners anyway.	I'd love to go. But why get bent out of shape about it? I can have a nice dinner with anyone I want to.
The hell with it all.	I admit, there has been a slow economy. I can stop overreacting. Life involves much more than one executive dinner. I can love and accept myself even though I can't always get my way.

RESULTS: Jack's written appraisal of his automatic and distorted self-talk leads to a more realistic view of reality and himself. The process of self-management has helped Jack to put an end to his negative feelings. He has solved the internal conflict and begins to feel good about himself, his company, and his job.

makes me work too hard. This takes some of the fun out of my job and my personal life. This belief system creates the illusion that work is life's only satisfaction. There are many other activities that I enjoy."

Conclusion

"I don't have to connect my self-esteem to my performance. I can do a good job in selling life insurance *and* enjoy my life. My new belief system is, 'My worth as a human being does not depend on the sales I make, the dollars I earn, or the recognition I get. My worth as a human being can't be earned, or be given to me by others. I'll give it to myself unconditionally. Then I can work with less emotional strain and more self-satisfaction. Feeling good all the way!'

Final Note

Writing your self-talk on paper appears deceptively simple, but it is actually very difficult. First, it requires action at a time where you may feel immobilized or overwhelmed by your negative feelings.

Second, it appears so illogical and unpromising. But the physical action of writing one's distorted self-talk on paper has the following benefits:

- Writing will prevent the automatic thoughts from endlessly repeating themselves in your mind.
- Writing will stop the process of building more internal chaos and negative feelings.
- Writing will show you (in your own handwriting) what hogwash you've been producing internally.

DR. DAVID BURNS: KEY IDEAS TO REMEMBER

1. Self-esteem is the ability to love or like yourself whether or not you are successful. Self-esteem is self-love. It doesn't have to be earned through achievement or perfection. You can give it to yourself without having to prove anything.

2. Your moods are created by your thoughts. By talking back to negative thoughts, you can often achieve a dramatic and positive change in your mood.

3. The most important step to managing your mood is to write your automatic (negative) thoughts on a piece of paper. The process of writing will stop the thoughts from repeating endlessly. The objective appraisal of your automatic self-talk will lead to a more realistic view of reality and yourself.

4. A belief system that says, "To be worthwhile, I must achieve," will reduce your effectiveness through unnecessary self-induced pressure. Perfectionist attitudes can contribute to lower performance and reduce a person's life and career satisfaction.

5. Overcome your negative, twisted, and distorted thought patterns, and you will boost your productivity and self-esteem.

Now please complete the Action Plan on the following page.

MY ACTION PLAN FOR SUCCESS

1.

2.

3.

4.

5.

7

Portrait of Negotiation:

GERARD I. NIERENBERG

Negotiation is so much a part of our daily lives that it is easy to take it for granted. Few of us ever bother to define a negotiation strategy; even fewer are consciously aware of our negotiation philosophy. Most of us employ a hit-and-miss strategy. By trying to get the best deal, we often leave the other person feeling bad or arrive at agreements that don't last. One thing is sure, not one of us ever wants to feel taken.

Gerard Nierenberg has spent a lifetime studying the subject of negotiation. He has defined negotiation climates, he has analyzed the importance of body language in negotiations, he has developed a unique process for finding a greater number of creative solutions, and much more. His negotiation philosophy is designed to lead to success for all parties. No one need ever feel like the loser in a Nierenberg negotiation, because everyone wins.

To me, that was a stunning concept. And, as I found long after our interview, his philosophy works. It works not only in selling or in business negotiations but also in relationships with parents, children, and spouses, and for anyone who has ever had to make a deal of any kind.

Nierenberg's guiding philosophy is, simply put, that the purpose of a good negotiation is not how to divide the remaining slice of pie. The purpose is how to make more pie for everyone.

It's a simple statement—deceptively simple. I discovered its practical benefits the very same evening that I interviewed Mr. Nierenberg.

My wife and I had reservations at the Watergate Hotel, one of Washington's best. When we arrived that night, the desk clerk informed me of a problem. She said that she could not find a room in the price category (the lowest rate) I had reserved. Remembering my studies of Nierenberg's climates of negotiation, I smiled at her, asking, "Would you consider this to be your problem or my problem?"

She quickly accepted the problem as her responsibility, so I proceeded: "I am pleased to hear you say that, and I feel positive that you'll do your best to find a solution that makes us both happy." I smiled again, this time nodding my head.

She repeated the nod and without hesitation handed me the key to the presidential suite, saying, "Would you be willing to stay tonight in our presidential suite at the price of our standard room?" We were beaming. We loved it. Two bedrooms, a spacious and elegantly appointed living room with an antique desk, a sweeping terrace overlooking the Potomac River, a kitchen with a well-stocked refrigerator, a large dining area, and two baths. Now I recommend the Watergate Hotel to everyone who visits Washington!

What's more, I realized that Nierenberg's negotiation philosophy was another major key to success.

It is a guiding philosophy that creates more for everyone, rather than dividing victor and vanquished. The consequences for business executives are staggering. Without the guiding philosophy of more for everyone, a negotiation will turn into a losing battle.

This is yet another instance in which the person shaped the philosophy and the philosophy shaped a Superachiever.

ARE YOU A GOOD NEGOTIATOR?

	YES	NO
1. Are you always aware of your own negotiation philosophy before you begin negotiating?	☐	☐
2. Have you ever taught another person how to negotiate?	☐	☐
3. Can you describe your ten best negotiating techniques?	☐	☐
4. When a negotiation has failed, can you pinpoint the reasons?	☐	☐

5. In negotiating, is it preferable to deal with
   someone with more negotiating experience
   than you have? . . . .   ☐   ☐

For the surprising answers, please turn to page 102

THE ART OF SALES NEGOTIATION

*"Your success as a sales professional," suggests Gerard
I. Nierenberg, "may well depend on your success as a negotiator." After spending a lifetime as a professional negotiator,
he authored the first book on the subject in 1968,* The Art of
Negotiating. *He founded the Negotiation Institute, Inc., in
New York City, and began a pioneering effort to define and
advance this critical business science. Mr. Nierenberg's advice and counsel are sought throughout the world wherever
he lectures for business and governments. "Many people
think they are sharp negotiators," says Mr. Nierenberg, who
now has six best-selling books to his credit, "when actually
they have only a small number of negotiating techniques at
their command."*

When Personal Selling Power *interviewed Mr. Nierenberg to learn more about how his negotiation experience
could be applied to selling, he quickly suggested widening
the focus, because "we are involved in negotiating in one
form or another each day of our lives." He illustrated his
point with this little anecdote: "A few years ago, the president of a large conglomerate came up to me after a seminar
on negotiating mergers and acquisitions. He said, 'Jerry,
we've been doing pretty well this year, and there is little you
can tell me about mergers and acquisitions. We know how to
make money. But you told me something important about
personal negotiations because I had a discussion with my
son before I left this morning, and he told me what I could do
with my whole conglomerate.'"*

**PSP: You are a lawyer by training. Did you learn
about negotiation in your legal practice?**

Nierenberg: This may surprise you, but legal expertise is no help in negotiation. Most lawyers have little training in negotiating other than their own experience. Lawyers are trained as adversaries. In an adversary relationship, you want to win. Practicing law only taught me that many legal victories have little to do with resolving a problem so that it stays resolved. Contracts that end up in court can turn a short-term winner quickly into a long-term loser.

PSP: What is the goal of a negotiation relationship compared to an adversary relationship?

Nierenberg: In a negotiation relationship, you want to resolve a problem so that it stays resolved. You want to create an agreement that lasts, where both parties remain satisfied in the long run. In a successful negotiation, everyone wins.

PSP: How can everyone win in a competitive society?

Nierenberg: The purpose of competition is to make everyone better, not to kill your competitor. If we would kill all our competitors, we would end up with an unproductive monopoly. Competition brings out the differences, and effective negotiation integrates these differences so that everyone gains. For example, in selling, your competitors teach you how to stay on your toes and remind you that they are going to do more for your customers if you don't do it.

PSP: You said once that negotiating is one of the least understood arts in human affairs. What are some of the discoveries you have made that could help us understand more about the negotiation process?

Nierenberg: Well, most people view negotiating as a process where two people are involved in dividing a slice of pie. Their main goal is to get the larger piece. After studying negotiation for more than seventeen years, we've come to the conclusion that the goal of a negotiation should not be how to divide the slice of pie but how to make more pie.

PSP: When did you create the Negotiation Institute, and how many people have you trained?

Nierenberg: We created the Negotiation Institute in 1966. Its purpose is to expand the knowledge of negotiation and to train negotiators. We do this through our public seminars, in-house seminars, and video and audio tapes. To date, in our public seminars alone, we've trained more than 115,000 people.

PSP: You've written several books on the subject. One of your books seems to suggest that we all have a negotiation philosophy whether we are aware of that philosophy or not. Is that correct?

Nierenberg: Yes. One of the strongest forces in our choosing one course of action over another is our philosophy. We need to look at our philosophy occasionally and find out how it is working for us. Our philosophy is made to serve us. We are not made to serve our philosophy.

PSP: Let's talk about the profession of selling. What type of philosophy would you recommend for a successful sales negotiation?

Nierenberg: A successful salesperson uses a problem-oriented philosophy. He or she views the prospect's problem as a mutual problem. He or she wants to plan *with* the client, not *for* the client. The other side of the coin would be the salesperson with the game-oriented philosophy. He or she views the prospect as an adversary, someone who must be controlled or manipulated. If you are trying to push or control your prospect, you will only increase his or her defenses and decrease your chances of making the sale.

PSP: You are talking about the emotional climate during a sale. How important are feelings in a sales negotiation?

Nierenberg: Let me answer with a question: How do you feel when you realize that the prospect is out to win and make you lose?

PSP: I probably would feel antagonized, competitive, or challenged.

Nierenberg: Right. Most people would react that

way. You see, in these situations, our emotional defense systems tend to take over. As a consequence, we are tempted to break off communication or want to make the other person lose.

PSP: *Do you feel we become responsible for the negative climate in this situation?*

Nierenberg: I would go further than that; *all* of the climates and feelings that we experience in the negotiating process are of our making.

PSP: *How can we control the climate in a sales negotiation?*

Nierenberg: If I am accusing, judgmental, correcting, or indoctrinating, I will most likely create a defensive prospect. For example, when I tell a prospect that my product is the best in the whole world . . . I am imposing a value judgment that will create a defensive climate.

PSP: *How can I avoid defensive reactions?*

Nierenberg: It's so easy. You can create a supportive climate by being descriptive. You could say, "Our product is currently used by 30,000 customers nationwide." Let the customer appraise your information; don't do it for him or her. Remember, customers want to learn, but they resist being taught.

PSP: *What if the prospect starts out being defensive?*

Nierenberg: It is much easier to change someone who is being defensive to you by being supportive to them, rather than by being defensive to them. You see, when we hit a tennis ball over the net, the kind of spin we put on the ball determines what type of return shot we are going to get. It's the same with negotiation climates. The type of climate you create determines the type of climate you're going to get.

PSP: *We've talked about how our philosophies influence our negotiations and how the climate contributes to the outcome. How important is nonverbal communication in the negotiation process?*

Nierenberg: It is a very important contributing factor. Most salespeople have only a limited awareness of the prospect's body language. The untrained sales negotiator may overlook as much as 50 percent of all nonverbal messages.

PSP: *How easily can we interpret a prospect's gestures?*

Nierenberg: A gesture does not mean anything by itself, unless we put it into a context. In order to understand what's going on, we must observe what I call a cluster or group of gestures. We need to watch out for the many shifts and changes before we can see the prospect move from one attitude to another. Also, we need to compare the nonverbal messages to what is said verbally so we can find out if the prospect's body is confirming or denying his or her verbal expressions.

PSP: *What if the prospect's gestures are inconsistent with the verbal message?*

Nierenberg: The nonverbal expression will give you the prospect's true attitude.

PSP: *What can we do when we realize that our own bodies communicate a defensive attitude? How can we change it?*

Nierenberg: By changing our feelings, we'll automatically change our body language. It's important to read our own gestures during a negotiation. They tell us how we feel, so we can examine the underlying causes. Once we realize what contributed to our defensive attitude, we can go ahead and change it.

PSP: *How about negotiations on the telephone, where we can't see the prospect's body language?*

Nierenberg: Francis Bacon said once, long before the telephone was invented, "If you have something important to communicate, don't write." I say, if you have something important to negotiate, don't call.

PSP: *Do you feel that people are more impulsive on the telephone than in person?*

Nierenberg: No, but we do things on the telephone we never would do in person. It's like when you get behind the wheel of a car and do things to other people that you would never do face to face. Some people are afraid on the telephone, some people become preoccupied with the expense of the call, and others become rash and rude and hang up.

PSP: In your book, The Art of Negotiating, *you describe many different negotiation techniques like "apparent withdrawal," "feinting," the "salami tactic," or the "crossroads strategy." These techniques sound like guidelines for a game, and yet in your seminars you say that negotiation and life are not games. Aren't you contradicting yourself?*

Nierenberg: Let me clarify this point for you. In a game, you have a limited number of alternatives. In a negotiation, you have an infinite number of alternatives. Games can be played over again, and players can be substituted. Life can't be played over. The rules of a game are given. But what do we know about the rules of life? Think about the many rules prospects make up during a negotiation. Or think about how many prospects actually subscribe to their own rules. Negotiation is not a simple process of sacrificing for the sake of agreement. Negotiation is not an infantile "let's split the difference" proposition. Negotiation is a process of maximizing our interests.

PSP: In other words, the experienced negotiator does not view the negotiating process as an "I win— you lose" game.

Nierenberg: Exactly. Amateurs want to play games; professionals want to solve problems so they stay solved.

PSP: What is your measure of success?

Nierenberg: To be able to pass on some of my own experiences.

ANSWERS TO QUIZ ON PAGE 95

1. Good negotiators are aware of their negotiation philosophy before they enter a negotiation. Research at the Negotiation Institute has shown that the outcome of any negotiation depends on our negotiating philosophy.

2. If you can teach your own negotiation techniques to someone else, you're already past the amateur status.

3. The inexperienced negotiator knows or uses only a handful of negotiation techniques. Good negotiators sharpen their skills and learn new techniques on an ongoing basis.

4. The inexperienced negotiator rationalizes failures by saying, "I don't want to do business with that type of person anymore." Good negotiators examine their failures and learn to pinpoint and avoid poor negotiating techniques.

5. Inexperienced negotiators want to deal with people who have less experience in negotiating. Experienced negotiators want to deal with people who have more experience. The object of negotiating is to come to a lasting agreement. Someone with more experience will more likely come up with more alternatives that lead to better solutions.

How to Interpret Your Score

Five Yes Answers: You are a good negotiator, and you'll enjoy reading Mr. Nierenberg's latest ideas on negotiating.

Four or Less Yes Answers: Congratulations! You'll benefit most from reading our interview with Mr. Nierenberg, a master negotiator.

SEVEN KEYS TO CREATE POSITIVE CLIMATES IN SALES NEGOTIATIONS

Gerard I. Nierenberg

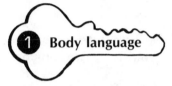

Avoid using gestures that are inconsistent with what is said. Don't fake an open attitude by grinning and manipulating your body language. Unless you are a great actor, you'll never get away with it. By the time your mind thinks what body language would be appropriate, it will be too late. You'll look like an actor in a dubbed foreign movie, your gestures will be behind the spoken word. Remember, genuine gestures *precede* the spoken word.

Be open minded to all potential strategies and tactics. Avoid limiting yourself to the strategies and tactics that have merely worked before.

Use questions to establish your prospect's needs, to clarify issues, to consider new alternatives. Effective questions channel thoughts, guide the discussions, and lead to greater understanding. Avoid questions that create anxiety. (Example: How can anyone say that we don't have a good product?)

Listen carefully. Evaluate the prospect's statement before responding. Avoid interruptions or contradictions.

Communicate clearly. Avoid using technical terms and clichés. Your role is to clarify, not to obstruct. Complex language builds a barrier between you and your prospect.

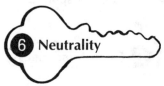

Avoid value judgments. Use neutral, descriptive terms. Don't assume the role of the teacher who indoctrinates. Assume the role of the explorer who helps the prospect discover a problem; then solve the problem together.

Avoid using either/or alternatives. Instead, develop creative alternatives. For example, to get away from the typical price negotiation, develop new alternatives like improved delivery, group price, package deal, extended terms, custom design, extra service, different deposits, customized payment plan, insurance for unknown losses, prevention of risks through new guarantees, letting the buyer produce some of the parts, allowing discounts for advance payments, and so on.

TEST YOUR NONVERBAL READING SKILLS

by Gerard I. Nierenberg

Study the buyer's nonverbal expressions carefully. Observe details such as hand signals, leg postures, body angle, and so on. You might even try to imitate the buyer's posture before choosing your answer among the four possible choices. Reading and responding to your buyer's silent language is one of the keys to a successful sales negotiation.

1.

Picture # 1. Nonverbal Expression	Mark the Correct Answer with an X
Uncertainty	☐
Superiority	☐
Defensiveness	☐
Evaluation	☐

2.

2.
Doubt	☐
Readiness	☐
Confidence	☐
Cooperation	☐

3.

3.
Nervousness ☐
Frustration ☐
Doubt ☐
Openness ☐

4.
Boredom
Superiority
Need for reassurance
Anger

4.
☐
☐
☐
☐

5.

5.
Uncertainty ☐
Disgust ☐
Thinking ☐
Frustration ☐

6.

6.
Offensive
Cooperation
Self-control
Lying

☐
☐
☐
☐

7.

7.
Honesty
Holding back
Readiness
Openness

☐
☐
☐
☐

8.

8.
Suspicion ☐
Acceptance ☐
Holding back ☐
Frustration ☐

9.
Relaxed
Defensive
Superiority
Expectancy

☐
☐
☐
☐

9.

10.

10.
Possessiveness ☐
Confidence ☐
Lying ☐
Pride ☐

11.
Expectancy ☐
Excitement ☐
Interest ☐
Interrupt sign ☐

11.

Answers

1. The prospect is *evaluating*. People who strike poses with one hand on their cheek are involved in some sort of meditation. A forward-leaning body indicates interest. Should the body be drawn back from you, the thought patterns can turn to suspicion.

2. The prospect joins his fingertips—a steepling gesture expressing *confidence*. It indicates the person is very sure of something. Research indicates that the more important the executive feels he or she is, the higher he or she tends to hold hands while steepling.

3. The prospect's index finger is touching the nose quickly, indicating *doubt*. Although the spoken words may indicate

otherwise, the signal is clear: "I am not buying!" A word of caution: A prospect rubbing his or her nose vigorously with a bent finger may simply do so because it itches.

4. The prospect's body is leaning back, holding both hands and knees signaling a *need for reassurance*. Take this opportunity to express reassurance and help the prospect to open up.

5. The prospect is supporting his head with both hands, communicating that he is *thinking*. If the gesture is followed by a shift back in a chair, the prospect's message can translate verbally into, "I am very sure of what I am thinking."

6. The prospect thrusts out his chin in response to an offensive message. His lips may tighten in a pursing gesture. It is advisable to respond to the *offensive sign* with a conciliatory message.

7. The prospect's coat is unbuttoned, his legs are uncrossed, and his arms appear relaxed. The upper body clearly shows openness. But wait. Look at his ankles, locked behind the chair. The prospect is *holding back,* waiting for you to earn more trust.

8. The prospect's hands are clasped and his ankles are locked. A typical *holding-back gesture* cluster. Don't use your trial closes on this prospect yet. Create new opportunities for him to open up.

9. The prospect appears *defensive*. His legs are crossed away from you, his arms are crossed, and his left hand is holding his right arm. His coat is buttoned. This is a typical defensive gesture cluster. Failure to recognize early signs of disagreement will usually lead to a more complicated situation.

10. The prospect is covering her mouth. When people conceal parts of their mouths while speaking, be careful. They may be *lying* or trying to cover up something. If a prospect makes a promise with his or her mouth covered, ask for it in writing.

11. The prospect is showing you his need to *interrupt* the conversation. Stop talking. Yield the floor. Learn to spot interrupt signals early and you will increase your sales success. (Nobody ever listened himself out of a sale!)

GERARD I. NIERENBERG: KEY IDEAS TO REMEMBER

1. The purpose of a good negotiation is not how to divide the remaining slice of pie. The purpose is how to make more pie for everyone.

2. The untrained negotiator may overlook as much as 50 percent of all nonverbal messages. Nonverbal expressions hold the key to the prospect's true attitude.

3. When we hit a tennis ball over the net, the kind of spin we put on the ball determines the type of return shot we are going to get. It's the same with negotiation climates. The type of climate you create determines the type of climate you're going to get.

4. It is easier to change someone's defensive attitude by being supportive rather than by echoing that person's defensiveness.

5. Amateurs want to play games; professionals want to solve problems so they stay solved.

Now please complete the Action Plan on the following page.

MY ACTION PLAN FOR SUCCESS

1.

2.

3.

4.

5.

8

Portrait of Financial Planning:

VENITA VANCASPEL

For Venita VanCaspel, dignity goes hand-in-hand with financial independence. One cannot exist without the other. For most Americans, financial independence is elusive or nonexistent. Ms. VanCaspel set out to fill a void in society, and she has been enormously successful. Her guiding philosophy—to help other people to retire with financial dignity—has paid off for her clients as well as for herself.

When Venita VanCaspel sought access to the financial world, she was rebuffed time and again. But she got the necessary training, did her apprenticeship, and then decided to become her own boss. It was a true Horatio Alger story, with the twist that it was a woman's determination to pursue her goals against all obstacles. Her rise in the world of financial planning has been steady.

On her national PBS television show, "Moneymakers," she gathers a forum of experts, along with a few plain folks who have questions about the workings of the financial maze. It was this show that introduced this versatile and energetic woman to me. I was impressed with the wealth of information, but most of all with the person. Venita VanCaspel is a woman with a mission. She is an expert when it comes to sales, but she also believes strongly in what she is selling. Financial independence is, for her, the most overlooked achievement in everyone's life.

Time and again I see evidence that she is right. I look at young people starting out, at middle-aged people who are halfway there, and at elderly people who no longer have recourse to planning ahead. A well-conceived, structured, and disciplined approach to financial planning in one's early or middle years can lead to a retirement that radiates the glow of a fulfilled life. I found her to be warm and caring, truly involved with the people she advised, and committed to the concept of financial independence for everyone.

This is yet another instance where one person's struggle to define the process of individual success has paid off in big dividends for many. Venita VanCaspel's philosophy governing the financial planning field can be put to work by anyone. When I showed this interview to my bookkeeper before publication, she said, "Where's her nearest branch office? And where do I sign?" To me, that says it all.

FIRST LADY OF FINANCIAL PLANNING

PSP: You said once that successful people are motivated by the desire for pleasing results, and people who fail are motivated by the desire for pleasing experiences. How did you come to that conclusion?

VanCaspel: Well, in my own life, I remember many instances where I would have preferred to have a good time instead of working for pleasing results. For instance, writing my first book was pure agony, and to this day I still don't enjoy writing, but I do enjoy the results from it. If I were looking for pleasing experiences, I would not have written a book; I would have gone out and played.

PSP: So you learned how to discipline yourself.

VanCaspel: Yes, if you want pleasing results, you need to give up the immediate pleasure.

PSP: As a financial planner, you are selling people on giving up immediate pleasure in order to reach financial independence. How did you learn how to sell?

VanCaspel: I don't think I was born with this ability, although my father was an automobile salesman. I find selling to be such a delight because, when you have a good product and make a sale, both you and your customer win. In the financial planning business there is a lot of responsibility riding on your ability to communicate. If you don't communicate well, perhaps a child won't be able to go to college, or a couple won't be able to retire in financial dignity. I feel this responsibility to be the key motivator for developing my sales abilities.

PSP: When did you start selling?

VanCaspel: I started as a little girl selling cosmetics and candy in a dime store. I worked after school and on weekends for long hours and very little pay. I grew up in Oklahoma. I remember everybody was very poor, and I picked cotton and peanuts to help make ends meet.

PSP: You also married a salesman.

VanCaspel: Yes, he sold advertising. We got married when I was in college. At that time, all I ever wanted to get out of life was a nice home, a husband, and children.

PSP: In your book, **The Power of Money Dynamics,** *you state, "Love is not so much looking into each other's eyes as looking in the same direction." Did you both look into the direction of financial independence?*

VanCaspel: I managed our money, and we saved a little on a regular basis. But we didn't have much knowledge of how to invest for financial independence.

PSP: How did you become an expert in this field?

VanCaspel: Well, it took a hard lesson to get me started. One day, back in 1959, I went to the airport in Dallas to pick up my husband, who had spent the day in Houston at a sales meeting. He had just been transferred to Dallas. It was a clear night; he was booked on a Braniff flight. The plane, an Electra carrying more than ninety passengers, had mechanical problems and crashed. There were no survivors. I tried to determine what to do with what was left of my life. I received some money from his insurance policy and decided to invest some of it in further education. I already had a degree in economics, but I didn't know how to invest money for financial independence. That's what I was determined to learn.

PSP: It sounds as if you have overcome one of the toughest struggles . . .

VanCaspel: It was tough. For a while, I asked the

question, "Why?" But you never make any progress until you move beyond that point. I remember praying, "Oh, God, give me a blueprint of what I am to do," until finally I accepted the fact that this isn't the way life works. You don't need the blueprint; you only need to know the next step. If you take that step, then you'll know the next one. It's like the person going down a dark trail with a lantern. He can't see the end of the trail in the darkness but has enough light to see the next step.

PSP: So your next step was to learn more about what to do with money.

VanCaspel: I took several investment courses where I learned that of every hundred persons who reach age sixty-five, only two are financially independent, twenty-three must continue working, and seventy-five must depend on friends, charity, or others. I felt a great need to help other people to retire with financial dignity. But after I got the proper education, I could not get a job with a brokerage firm in Houston.

PSP: You moved back to Houston?

VanCaspel: Yes, that's where all my friends were.

PSP: How many stockbrokers did you contact?

VanCaspel: I went to about fifteen firms, but nobody wanted to take a chance with a woman. One broker said, "We tried a woman once before, but it didn't work." Then I read the rules of the New York Stock Exchange and found that the only requirement for becoming a broker was to work for a member firm for a period of six months and to pass an exam. But the rules did not state what type of work you had to do for a member firm. So, I simply decided to take a job as a clerk with a brokerage firm and took a correspondence course with the New York Institute of Finance. Six months later, I asked to take the exam. They didn't think I would pass the exam, but I did. Then they said, "We'll throw you in the water and see if you can swim." I didn't get a draw like the men did, I didn't get any training, but I got a desk in the front office.

PSP: *How did you go about getting clients?*

VanCapel: I bought a book on cold calling and read it from cover to cover. One morning I went to the tallest building in Houston and started at the top floor, determined to work my way down, just as the book suggested. By noon I was so discouraged that I decided to quit. Nobody wanted to talk to me. Then I remembered a lecture given by a lady at a mutual funds seminar. She talked about how to create "a room full of prospects," and I realized that her method had more promise than all the cold-calling techniques in the world.

PSP: *If you can't get to see your prospects, get your prospects to see you.*

VanCaspel: That's exactly what I thought. So I went to see the executive director of the Chamber of Commerce and asked for the names of all the women's clubs in town. I asked my boss to write a letter to each club offering my services as a speaker. At that time I had no speaking experience. A few clubs invited me, and I began to get clients.

PSP: *Do you remember how many people attended when you gave your first presentation?*

VanCaspel: Nine people. After speaking to several women's clubs, I contacted a large department store. I thought that this was a good way to attract more traffic to the store and more prospects to my company. So we put ads in the paper. People came, and the crowds grew in size to a point where we had to limit the registration. Then one day the department store could not have me because of a special show they had organized. So I held my presentation at a hotel, and the audience was twice as large.

PSP: *You realized that the main attraction was not the department store . . .*

VanCaspel: Yes, and I never went back to the department store again.

PSP: *How did your male colleagues react to your new prospecting and selling methods?*

VanCaspel: Well, they put me in a new branch office

and expected it to be in the red for the first two years, but I put it into the black the first month. The business was growing so fast that I could not handle all the paperwork. I asked for a secretary, but they said no. Then I asked if I could hire one if I paid her salary out of my pocket, and they said, "Yes, you can, but we need to pay 10 percent of her salary because we want to have her under our control."

PSP: *How many brokers did the firm employ at that time?*

VanCaspel: About thirty-five. I became their top producer after only a few weeks.

PSP: *Did this motivate you to go out on your own?*

VanCaspel: The real motivation to start my own business came through the realization that my clients really needed someone to sit down with and develop a total financial plan. I realized that all brokers would do would be to persuade their clients to put all their money into equity. Insurance agents would suggest to their prospects that they put all their money in whole life policies. And CPAs would tell them how much they owed on taxes but not necessarily how to reduce taxes. I wanted to serve my clients' needs for better overall financial planning. I wanted to put my arms around them and hold them, saying, "Here is where we are now, here is where we want to go, and here are the choices for getting there." A lot of my friends supported my new philosophy, and when I opened my firm in 1968, on my very first day I did $1 million worth of business.

PSP: *Do you feel that there are more people who know how to earn a living than people who know how to invest and make their earnings work for them?*

VanCaspel: Only very few know now to make their earnings work for them. I don't think that wealthy people necessarily know what to do with their money. I just talked to a man today. His net worth was over $7 million, and he knows how to produce a good product and how to sell it, but he doesn't have the vaguest idea about how to invest his money.

PSP: You had a weekly TV show entitled "Successful Texans." What was the most important lesson you have learned from successful people?

VanCaspel: The one most common characteristic I found was that they knew where they were going. They all were determined to reach their goals and would not let any obstacle discourage them. I learned a great deal about my own life from interviewing them.

PSP: What is your measure of success?

VanCaspel: I enjoy it when my clients' assets increase and when they meet their financial goals.

PSP: How about your own goals?

VanCaspel: I love my company. I fought hard to keep it small because I don't get my kicks out of directing a lot of people.

PSP: That seems unusual. Many successful people seem to be proud of creating big monuments.

VanCaspel: I don't get hung up on that. Most of the time I am sort of surprised that people are impressed with what I do. I am also surprised that more people don't do what is so obvious to do. I constantly think about new ways to make money. There are so many possibilities out there. The world of money changes every day, and it's a big challenge for me always to be a step ahead.

PSP: You said once that it's so easy to succeed because so few are trying.

VanCaspel: Look around you. Do you see many people trying?

PSP: I see a lot of people working very hard and not going very far.

VanCaspel: There is a difference between activity and accomplishment. Most of them are just being active.

PSP: What makes it easier for you?

VanCaspel: I have a lot of good people working for me.

PSP: How do you invest your own money?

VanCaspel: I own several companies. I own the Diamond V Ranch, where I raise commercial cattle and race horses.

PSP: Do you consider racehorses to be a good investment?

VanCaspel: I decided to invest in a breeding operation when I read the 1981 tax bill. I found that racehorses offer a very favorable depreciation schedule. This cuts my taxes.

PSP: Have you ever paid taxes?

VanCaspel: Intelligent people don't pay taxes. Just kidding. I do pay some taxes. I consider tax savings through write-offs as a good use of money. I feel it is better to put money into job-producing investments than to run it through a wasteful bureaucracy. I feel good about direct investments in American ingenuity.

PSP: What is the key to a good investment philosophy?

VanCaspel: You never win by being a lender; you only win by being an owner. For example, owning a piece of American industry or real estate is a better bet than putting money into CDs or bonds.

PSP: What do you consider to be the key parts of a good investment plan?

VanCaspel: Agility and diversification. Don't put all your eggs into one basket. Create a plan that considers the time you have available, your tax situation, and the amount of assets you have to work with.

PSP: In your seminars, you talk about developing a winning attitude about money. What does money mean to you?

VanCaspel: It gives you options; that's all it does. It doesn't mean happiness.

PSP: What's the most common misunderstanding people have about money?

VanCaspel: Well, most people confuse stability with

safety. Stability means the same return of a number of dollars. Safety is the return of the same amount of food, clothing, and shelter. I suggest to my clients that they put their dollars in a safe position, not a stable position. In all my years of counseling, I never have found a quality, fixed-dollar investment with a high enough yield to accomplish long-term safety. The increase in the cost of living has always outpaced the return.

PSP: How do you change people's attitudes about money?

VanCaspel: Many people are reluctant to talk about money. I think it's dumb not to talk about it. Sometimes I feel that we are living in a world of financial illiterates because people regard money as a taboo subject.

PSP: Do you think this is true for both men and women?

Van Caspel: It's generally true for both. I do, however, encourage women to become more assertive about money. I tell them that the first thing I want them to understand is that I do not feel it is one of their inalienable rights to expect some man to take care of them financially. If you are married, you need to be a partner and work with your husband toward financial independence. Don't buy the old idea that it is not nice to talk about money; it has no place in today's world. If you don't talk about money, you won't have any money.

PSP: You are selling your clients on reaching financial independence. What exactly do you mean by that?

VanCaspel: It means different things to different people. In general, I suggest setting the initial goal at about $300,000.

PSP: Do you remember how many of your clients who started with your firm in 1968 have achieved financial independence?

VanCaspel: Oh, everybody who has stuck with me has. There is no magic about it; if you follow my program of saving so much every month and doing what I tell you to do, you are going to make it. I take little risk. I had a couple come in a while back saying, "We just came by to thank you. We never ever dreamed we would have that much money." They also told me that they had more fun saving and investing their money than spending it. That makes me feel good.

PSP: What's the first step in reaching financial independence?

VanCaspel: First, you must save 10 percent of all you earn and not touch the interest from it until you become financially independent. Don't invest everything in today's goods and services; save some for tomorrow's goods and services.

PSP: Why do most people fail to follow a plan for reaching financial independence?

VanCaspel: First, they think they have plenty of time on their hands, so they don't have to worry. Second, they fail to establish a goal. Third, they don't understand what money can do for them.

PSP: Which one of these three reasons would you consider as the most important roadblock?

VanCaspel: Procrastination. They think they have an unlimited amount of time on their hands.

PSP: How do you handle your own clients when they show signs of procrastination?

VanCaspel: I begin to deal with that subject when people come to my seminar. I explain that the best financial plan in the world is useless unless they do something about it. When they come to my office, they receive all the information they need to make the decision. If they want to delay the decision, I take the attitude that they are not saying, "No," but "Tell me more." If there is enough time, I go over the entire plan a second time. I also try to prevent people from procrastinating by offering alternatives. I don't ask my clients how much money they want to invest, but I ask them how much money they want to keep idle. I outline the plan and then ask if they like the diversification.

PSP: You ask your clients to make a number of minor decisions?

VanCaspel: Right. Most people don't seem to want to make decisions. They want you to make the decisions for them.

PSP: You said earlier that many people feel uncomfortable talking about money. How do you put them at ease?

VanCaspel: We start with our office design. We deliberately furnished it so it looks like a home. My desk doesn't have corners; there is an overhang so clients can put their feet underneath. My planners all use round tables to avoid barriers. Body language is so important. Clients don't want to be impressed by a star; they want to be close to you, be a part of you. They want to find somebody they can trust.

PSP: How do you establish trust?

VanCaspel: You achieve this with an open attitude, you avoid using notes, you look into their eyes, you study their faces, and you avoid any barriers between you and your audience or client.

PSP: Do you use humor?

VanCaspel: I don't tell jokes, but I say things in a way that makes you laugh about a serious subject. I believe that if you can't laugh about it, you can't change it. For example, in my seminars I suggest keeping a certain amount of money idle to give you peace of mind. I say, "People need pattin' money," and I pat an imaginary pile of money. "Pattin' money gives you peace of mind, and peace of mind is a good investment." A lot of people come into my office saying that they have too much pattin' money. They would have never made that move unless they first laughed about it. You have to get people to laugh about a serious subject, or they won't change.

PSP: Do you feel you are an entertainer?

VanCaspel: I know it is a performance, but it is for their own good. I think I am the poor man's Carol Burnett.

PSP: *I think you're the first lady of financial planning.*

VanCaspel: Thank you for the compliment.

VENITA VANCASPEL: KEY IDEAS TO REMEMBER

1. The best financial plan in the world is useless unless you follow through with action.

2. Save 10 percent of all you earn, and do not touch the interest from it until you become financially independent.

3. If you are married, you need to be a partner and work with your husband or wife toward financial independence. Don't buy the old idea that it is not nice to talk about money; it has no place in today's world. If you don't talk about money, you won't have any money.

4. The most common characteristic of successful people is that they know where they are going. They are determined to reach their goals and won't let any obstacle discourage them.

5. Successful people are motivated by the desire for pleasing results. People who fail are motivated by the desire for pleasing experiences.

Now please complete the Action Plan on the following page.

MY ACTION PLAN FOR SUCCESS

1.

2.

3.

4.

5.

9

Portrait of Physical Fitness:

DR. KENNETH H. COOPER

We were all far more physically active as children than we are as adults. Staying in shape or getting back in shape is a wholly grownup notion. But so is the way we let ourselves get out of shape.

For Dr. Kenneth H. Cooper, methodical physical exercise is the guiding philosophy by which he lives.

Dr. Cooper didn't come to his view of fitness and wellbeing without experiencing problems or pain. At one time he was as out of shape as any of us. It took a frightening experience on water skis to show him just how important physical fitness is.

Dr. Cooper's concept of fitness and the enormous body of clinical evidence to support it is impressive. Physical fitness, he asserts, begins on the inside, with our cardiovascular system. It is neither cosmetic nor transitory. Fitness can't be stored. Fitness is the result of ongoing, concentrated aerobic activity along with proper dietary balance.

In large part, Dr. Ken Cooper is responsible for the fitness movement that has swept this country during the past decade. His tireless work with countless patients, along with his internationally renowned fitness center in Dallas, have put physical fitness on the map for good.

No one can deny the benefits of being physically fit as we embark on our journey to success. Only regular exercise can help us truly understand how physical fitness and success are intertwined. Most Superachievers I've talked to told me that they have established a personal physical exercise routine. Dr. Wayne Dyer, Zig Ziglar, and Dr. David Burns are enthusiastic joggers. Dr. Norman Vincent Peale loves to walk; Venita VanCaspel also likes to walk as well as running or jumping on a trampoline. Everyone knows how much Ronald Reagan enjoys horseback riding. They have all chosen a physically active life. (As the exception, Senator Sam Ervin Jr., never seemed to pay particular attention to physical activity, and he's approaching his eighty-eighth birthday at the time of this writing.)

Dr. Cooper's experience with thousands of people of all ages, combined with his extensive scientific research, build a strong case that an ongoing aerobic exercise program will ultimately put the odds in your favor.

Sold by Dr. Cooper's evidence, I decided to follow his advice and began to walk regularly four times a week. It has become a pleasant routine that I now look forward to, since I enjoy the tangible benefits of a clear mind, improved concentration, reduced stress, and normal blood pressure.

I am convinced that Dr. Cooper's philosophy of physical fitness from the inside out can create the foundation for a more successful you.

ARE YOU FIT FOR SUCCESS?

Fifteen years ago, as a member of the U.S. Air Force Medical Corps, Dr. Cooper created the first comprehensive aerobic fitness program. "I could not sell it," he concedes today, "to anybody."

Convinced that he had found the key to total well-being, he left the safety of a very promising career in the military and moved to Dallas.

He succeeded in borrowing funds to invest in a medical practice. The first two years, he did not receive much support from the medical community, and only a few clients found their way to his office. "I thought that people would come in droves, but I was in for a real surprise," says Dr. Cooper, reflecting on his startup period. "I seriously considered giving up. I thought it was not worth it."

Today, Dr. Cooper's Aerobic Center is spread out over twenty-seven acres of prime land in Dallas. Each day, more than 1300 people come to exercise in this ultramodern center.

His books have been translated into twenty-nine languages and have sold more than 12 million copies. In Brazil, people refer to jogging as "doing their Cooper."

At fifty-one, Dr. Cooper enjoys his worldwide success. A Japanese syndicate has retained his services for developing a modern aerobics center on 750 acres near Tokyo. He receives invitations from every corner of the globe to help build aerobics centers based on the advanced concepts developed in Dallas.

Dr. Cooper has sold thousands on the benefits of physical fitness. His salesmanship goes far beyond the amateur level instilled in medical schools. Sometimes he even resorts to quoting Plato to persuade a hesitant patient: "Lack of activity destroys the good condition of every human being, while movement and methodical physical exercise save and preserve it."

After our interview, I checked up on Plato and found to my surprise that the Greek philosopher took his own advice and lived longer than the average American male. He lived—2300 years ago—to the fit and active age of eighty!

PSP: Before this interview, we surveyed a small number of sales executives about their health habits. We found that the ones who do not exercise regularly are not only overweight but also tend to feel guilty about their self-defeating attitudes. They all agree on the benefits of fitness, but they procrastinate and don't take positive action.

Dr. Cooper: I've seen many people with this attitude. They say, "I am just going to take my chances. I want to enjoy life to the fullest."

PSP: Eating brownies while they watch Richard Simmons...

Dr. Cooper: Right, but they also want to be successful in life and overlook that the important thing for achieving success is good health. I haven't missed a day at work in twenty-three years because of illness.

PSP: In your book, The Aerobics Program for

Total Wellness, you admitted that you yourself did not always practice good health habits.

Dr. Cooper: That's right. I thought, like so many people, that I didn't have to worry about my calorie intake. I was totally disinterested in any type of physical activity. I thought I could ignore all the recommendations about health because I had some inborn immunity. That's the type of rationalization I used.

PSP: You were overweight?

Dr. Cooper: Yes, during my medical training I gained at least thirty pounds. The big problem occurred during my internship in Seattle. We were working late every night, and we just ate to keep awake. There was a snack bar. It was open all night and free to the hospital staff.

PSP: That's hard to resist.

Dr. Cooper: We were so busy and didn't have the time to exercise, so by the time I finished my internship I had gained a lot of weight.

PSP: That was before you joined the Army?

Dr. Cooper: I joined the Army in August 1957 and went to some training programs but was still quite overweight. When I got married in August of 1959, my wife started cooking and I became even more lethargic. I remember saying to her, "I feel like I am dying of mental stagnation."

PSP: Was that from your lack of activity?

Dr. Cooper: It was probably as much physical as it was mental. I kind of felt that there was nothing to challenge me. I had anticipated spending just two years in the military and then pursuing an orthopedic residency or specializing in ophthalmology. But once I got into the military, I didn't pursue either one of those goals.

PSP: What prompted you to get out of your mental stagnation?

Dr. Cooper: I decided to make a career change and got interested in aviation and aerospace medicine. So I transferred to the Air Force.

PSP: Did this change your attitude about physical fitness?

Dr. Cooper: No, the experience that had the greatest impact on me was one single incident while I was water skiing. I had no idea what an extra thirty pounds could do to my body. I put on a slalom ski after many years of deconditioning, and I told the driver to accelerate to thirty miles per hour. To my surprise, after only a few minutes, I began to feel nauseated and weak. I told the driver to get me back, and for a half-hour I lay on the shore in agony. My head was spinning and I was unable to put a series of logical thoughts together. I suspect that I suffered some type of cardiac arrhythmia. My heart had been stimulated beyond its capacity and was beating very fast and out of control.

PSP: A frightening experience...

Dr. Cooper: It really frightened me, and I became so depressed about my physical deterioration that I began to change my life-style. I reduced my weight and exercised regularly.

PSP: Dr. Cooper, not everyone has an emotionally significant experience to push them into action. How do you sell people on committing themselves to physical fitness?

Dr. Cooper: I am not convinced that even near-death experiences have a long-term effect on many people. At the Aerobics Center we use a proper balance of education and motivation. We have very exciting, motivated leaders. Our members attend different classes and they benefit from an award system.

PSP: You reward them for their progress?

Dr. Cooper: Yes, we have the 100 Mile Club, the 1000, the 5000, and the 10,000 Mile Clubs. We want our members to be aware of their progress. We use constant encouragement, objective feedback, and continuous goal setting.

PSP: How many people come here to exercise?

Dr. Cooper: About 1300 people exercise here every

day. We now have a fourteen-month waiting list for people who want to join our center.

PSP: What do you mean by being physically fit? Do you have an objective way to measure fitness?

Dr. Cooper: Historically, physicians have classified their patients as being physically fit if they are free from disease. A weight lifter may say it means having bulging muscles; a young lady might say it means having a lovely figure. To me, physical fitness means a good cardiovascular–pulmonary system, which means that you are fit for life. I suggest to focus on the organs you live with first. Once you've built your cardiovascular reserves and achieved fitness on the inside, then you begin to work on the outside, the muscle building or figure contouring.

PSP: So your priorities are, first, fit for life and second, fit for looks.

Dr. Cooper: Yes, what I am saying is that the weight lifting and the figure tone-ups are great but should be done in conjunction with, not in place of, aerobic exercise.

PSP: What exactly does aerobics mean?

Dr. Cooper: It literally means exercising with air and refers primarily to endurance types of exercise.

PSP: What type of exercise would qualify?

Dr. Cooper: Some people prefer to jog; others walk, swim, dance, play tennis, or ride a bike.

PSP: Does each activity lead to the same level of fitness?

Dr. Cooper: It doesn't make a difference what type of aerobic exercise you engage in; the key is to increase your heart rate for a period of at least twenty minutes.

PSP: How many times a week?

Dr. Cooper: We encourage people to work a minimum of thirty minutes three times a week or twenty minutes four times a week.

PSP: So you don't need to run fifteen miles every day?

Dr. Cooper: No, fifteen miles a week is the optimum.

If you run more than fifteen miles per week, you are running for something other than cardiovascular fitness.

PSP: How can you test your level of fitness without going through your stress tests?

Dr. Cooper: I use a very simple test in my presentations. I ask the audience to count their pulse for fifteen seconds and then multiply that figure by four to get the number of heartbeats per minute. Then I ask for a show of hands. In a group of 400 there is usually one person with a resting heart rate of less than fifty, which we consider as athletic. Fifty to sixty is excellent; sixty to seventy is good. Seventy to eighty is average; most American men and women are within this category. Eighty to ninety is fair, and over ninety is poor.

PSP: How soon after you begin an aerobics exercise program can you expect a lower resting pulse as a result?

Dr. Cooper: Well, our studies have shown that, for example, middle-aged men between forty-five and fifty-five years of age had an average heart rate of seventy-two beats per minute. After three months of conditioning, the average rate was fifty-five beats per minute. If you were to start exercising today, you'd notice some changes within eight weeks and a significant change by the twelfth week.

PSP: Zig Ziglar said once, "The tougher you are on yourself, the easier life will be on you."

Dr. Cooper: Exactly. Zig is a classic example of what a person can do. He has gone from total inactivity and weighing about thirty pounds more than he weighs at the present time, to the top percentile of all people who have come here. He stayed longer on the treadmill than any professional football player we've ever had in our center.

PSP: And he's past fifty-five years old.

Dr. Cooper: Yes, he's a prime example of what a positive attitude toward fitness can do.

PSP: Zig started out by walking and added a little jogging each day.

Dr. Cooper: That's the beauty of the aerobic system;

you can choose the fitness level you want to achieve by selecting the intensity and duration of activity.

PSP: Do you find that aerobic exercise reduces stress and anxiety?

Dr. Cooper: I think it is nature's best tranquilizer. I have a very busy schedule; today is a classic example. I have been here since six-thirty in the morning, I took only ten minutes for lunch, I've been constantly involved with patients. If I go home tonight without working out, I won't sleep well. I will take the activities of the day home with me, and they will run over in my mind all night long. I'll toss and turn and be very keyed up. But if I go out and run two or three miles, as I will before I go home this evening, I will come home totally relaxed.

PSP: How do you explain this relaxing effect?

Dr. Cooper: During a stressful day, your adrenal system produces hormones that set you up for flight-or-fight responses. You are keyed up from a high level of these hormones. Your body can't relax until this chemical imbalance is corrected. Exercise helps you dissipate the stress, and you end up feeling refreshed and relaxed. If you don't allow for a physiological release, you tend to respond to your body's demand for chemical balance by having a drink or taking a tranquilizer.

PSP: So you are essentially saying that if you invest in aerobic exercise, your internal system is working smarter, not harder.

Dr. Cooper: Yes, and there are a number of additional benefits, such as higher enthusiasm, better energy levels, higher confidence, and improved attitudes.

PSP: Have you been able to measure an increase in productivity on the job because of exercise?

Dr. Cooper: There are numerous cases that document lower health insurance premiums as a result of company fitness programs. We recently conducted an extensive study involving 7400 teachers in Dallas where the participants of a regular exercise program had fewer sick days during the school year. By figuring the direct cost saved on substitute teachers alone, we could document a savings of $452,000.

PSP: Have you designed company fitness programs?

Dr. Cooper: We've worked with many corporations. One of the first was Xerox. There is an increased consciousness about the value of fitness throughout the world. For example, IBM spent more than $1 million last year involving more than 40,000 people in a wellness program.

PSP: How about overseas?

Dr. Cooper: I just got back from Tokyo. The Japanese are building the Nihon Aerobic Center on 750 acres following the know-how we've developed here in Dallas. In Brazil, since 1970, people have referred to their jogging as "doing their Cooper." We receive invitations from every corner of the globe. Just this week I received an invitation to help an organization build a center in Egypt, another request came from Malaysia, and last week I received two invitations from Australia.

PSP: You are traveling extensively. What do you recommend to traveling salespeople? How can you maintain a healthy diet when you are on the road, passing hundreds of fast-food places...

Dr. Cooper: I have the same problem salespeople have. Sometimes I skip meals. I know this is not ideal, but I can't eat a big meal before giving a speech. Our staff nutritionist just finished this little brochure with tips on selecting items in fast-food restaurants. (See page 143.)

PSP: What do you consider to be the dangers of an extra ten or fifteen pounds?

Dr. Cooper: Your risk of having a heart attack is greater. New scientific evidence prompted me to reverse the statement I have used over the years, saying that "exercise can overcome many, if not all, the deleterious effects of diet." We've been able to study a number of people who exercise properly but ignored their twenty pounds of extra weight and suffered from a heart attack later on.

PSP: So, aerobics alone is no guarantee.

Dr. Cooper: A combination of exercise and diet reduces your risks much more.

PSP: You said once that when a person dies, he dies not so much of the particular disease as of his entire life.

Dr. Cooper: True. I am convinced that the leading causes of death in the prime of life are more acts of man than acts of God.

PSP: How can you improve your chances for losing weight? What solution do you have in addition to exercising and limiting calories?

Dr. Cooper: I suggest that overweight salespeople eat 75 percent of their daily calories before one o'clock p.m. Try to eat 25 percent at breakfast, 50 percent at lunch, and 25 percent at dinner.

PSP: Take your client out to lunch and avoid entertaining in the evening.

Dr. Cooper: Right. We have done a study involving two groups of overweight people who were consuming 1200 calories per day. The group that consumed 75 percent of their calories before one o'clock p.m. lost a great deal more weight.

PSP: Why?

Dr. Cooper: We are not sure, but I suspect that if you take in most of your food early in the day your body remains relatively active during the digestive process.

PSP: You also recommend exercising before your evening meal?

Dr. Cooper: Yes, this reduces your appetite and leads you to eat less.

PSP: How about taking a shortcut with a low-calorie diet?

Dr. Cooper: Dr. Katahn, author of the book *The 200 Calorie Solution,* talks about these shortcuts. A low-calorie diet can help you lose weight rapidly, but you will gain it back just as fast, only with fewer calories than it took to maintain your weight before.

PSP: Why is that?

Dr. Cooper: Let's say your metabolism requires 2000 calories per day. If you go on a 300-calorie diet, you may lose as much as fifteen pounds in three weeks. As a response to this lower caloric intake, your body lowers the metabolism. After three weeks, your metabolism may have dropped from 2000 to 1200 calories. As soon as you get off your low-calorie diet, your weight will go up rapidly, even if you eat less, let's say only 1600 calories.

PSP: When does your reduced metabolism go back to the previous level?

Dr. Cooper: It takes a long time, perhaps as long as a year to readjust your metabolism back to the original level.

PSP: So the shortcut doesn't seem to solve the problem over the long run.

Dr. Cooper: No.

PSP: You said earlier that health is an important criterion for achieving success. What is your measure of success?

Dr. Cooper: To enjoy what I am doing. I think that is a very important factor of success. I set high goals for myself, and once I reach those goals I establish new ones. The Aerobics Center has expanded much farther than I ever dreamed it would.

PSP: What were the low points on your way to success?

Dr. Cooper Well, there are a couple of low points. First, the criticism I received back in the Air Force from my peers and colleagues when I tried to promote my fitness program.

PSP: How did you overcome this setback?

Dr. Cooper: Well, I refused to accept anything that would slow me down. I kept my sights right ahead. I refused to buckle.

PSP: You were loyal to your dreams.

Dr. Cooper: Yes, and it required time. The way I overcame that obstacle was by doubling my efforts. I began to write books, undertook research projects, and searched for answers. I wouldn't accept the statement that jogging is bad and people should not do it. But it was up to me to find solutions until, finally, the Air Force began to accept my concepts.

PSP: What was the second lowest point?

Dr. Cooper: Well, without question, the second lowest point came right after our office was established in Dallas. I thought that people would come in droves. I hoped for the acceptance of the medical community here in Dallas. But I was in for a real surprise. It was very, very difficult. For the first couple of years I seriously considered giving up. I thought it was not worth it.

PSP: You thought you had it made after leaving the Air Force.

Dr. Cooper: At age forty, I left what could have been a very promising career and started completely from scratch. I didn't have a leg to stand on, I moved into a new community, my wife was pregnant, and I had no insurance, no place to work, no home to live in, and no money.

PSP: And little support from the medical community.

Dr. Cooper: Support wasn't coming, people were not coming in, so after two years I was convinced that I'd made a mistake and considered going back to the Air Force.

PSP: What caused you to stay?

Dr. Cooper: I have to give credit to my wife. She really encouraged me to stay in the field, to tough it out. The worst years were 1971 and 1972. Then it started to turn around. In 1972, Frank Shorter, the marathon runner, won the gold medal in the Olympics in Munich. He created a national interest and pride in running. More and more people began to get involved in running. In the late 1960s, there were only about 100,000 joggers in this country compared to more than 20 million today.

PSP: It sounds like your persistence paid off.

Dr. Cooper: Of course, there were other factors in my

success, like the willingness to work. I still put in twelve- to fourteen-hour days.

PSP: *Your enthusiasm in selling your program was probably a large factor, too.*

Dr. Cooper: That's right, because it takes a lot of selling to convince people that it is a whole lot cheaper and more effective to maintain good health than to regain it once it's gone.

TIPS FOR ORDERING IN FAST-FOOD RESTAURANTS:
by Dr. Kenneth H. Cooper

1. Avoid desserts, sweets, milk shakes, pies, and cookies.
2. Split a sandwich with a friend.
3. Omit mayonnaise from the sandwich. Ask to hold the cheese. (One teaspoon of mayonnaise provides 100 calories. One ounce of cheese also provides 100 calories).
4. Order an open-face sandwich or eat only half the bun.
5. Avoid high-calorie beverages. For example, a milk shake can add 400 calories to your lunch, a regular soft drink only 50.
6. Order low-fat milk, low-calorie soft drinks, fruit juices, or water.
7. Avoid fried foods, because calories can more than double in foods that are deep fried. If you can't resist, remove the outer crust before eating.
8. If you order pizza, order a small size with cheese only. Extra toppings with low-calorie contents are green peppers, onions, and mushrooms.
9. Order a huge salad. Fill up on lettuce, tomatoes, mushrooms, green peppers, carrots, celery, and cucumbers. Limit your intake of ham, croutons, kidney beans, cheese, nuts, and bacon bits. Avoid creamy dressings. Use oil and vinegar.
10. Carry some fresh fruit with you to eat as dessert.

11. If you are trying to cut down on sodium, try to avoid fast food completely. For example, a Whopper sandwich contains 990 milligrams of sodium. Order french fries without salt. Several fast-food chains accept special salt-free orders on short notice (telephone reservation).

DR. KENNETH COOPER: KEY IDEAS TO REMEMBER

1. Physical fitness can't be stored. Fitness is the result of ongoing, concentrated aerobic activity along with proper dietary balance.

2. Aerobic exercise builds cardiovascular–pulmonary fitness. Once you've achieved fitness on the inside, then you begin to work on the outside, the muscle building or figure contouring.

3. When a person dies, he dies not so much of the particular disease as of his entire life.

4. During a stressful day, your adrenal system produces hormones that set you up for flight-or-fight responses. You are keyed up from a high level of these hormones. Your body can't relax until this chemical imbalance is corrected. Exercise helps you dissipate the stress, and you end up feeling refreshed and relaxed. Aerobic exercise is nature's best tranquilizer.

5. It doesn't make a difference what type of aerobic exercise you engage in; the key is to increase your heart rate for a period of at least twenty minutes. You can choose to work a minimum of thirty minutes three times a week or twenty minutes four times a week.

   Now please complete the Action Plan on the following page.

MY ACTION PLAN FOR SUCCESS

1.

2.

3.

4.

5.

10

Portrait of Integrity:

SENATOR
SAM J. ERVIN JR.

Former Senator Sam J. Ervin Jr.'s life is characterized by his fidelity to the truth. His insights are profound and illuminating.

"Our greatest possession is not the vast domain, it's not our beautiful mountains, or our fertile prairies, or our magnificent coastline," he lectures in front of a spellbound audience. "It's not the might of our Army or Navy. These things are of great importance. But, in my judgment, the greatest and most precious possession of the American people is the Constitution." Sam Ervin has dedicated himself to the Constitution and the truth he sees in it.

Sam Ervin's love for the Constitution finds its only rival in his love for his wife Margaret.

His guiding philosophies have been shaped by advice from his parents and his teachers and by his determination to learn from the lessons of history.

His mother gently guided his attitudes about dealing with people when she said, "There is a lot of good in everybody, and the most foolish thing a person can do is try to reform another. You can't reform other people, but you can try to call out the best qualities in them and try to see that they exercise those."

It was his father who taught him the meaning of integrity by example, with these words: "Never tell a lie. Even when it damages you, always tell the truth."

During the nationally televised Watergate hearings, Senator Ervin lit up many faces by emphasizing the widespread lack of loyalty to the truth: "What's right is right, and what's wrong is wrong, and you can't compromise with integrity."

In a delightful Columbia record entitled *Senator Sam at Home,* he shows his love for the English language, poetry, and simple country wisdom. The record, no longer available in stores, is now a collector's item. It contains a precious sampling of Ervin's keen sense of humor and down-to-earth philosophies.

When I listened to this record in the Library of Congress, I heard a soft and gentlemanly voice masking a sharp and clear mind, speaking about the meaning of defeat with words I shall never forget: "Defeat may serve as well as victory to shake the soul and let the glory out."

Never before have I seen a clearer example of how a person's guiding philosophy shapes his destiny. After returning from Morganton, North Carolina, I checked Sam Ervin's definition of a leader with that of Richard Nixon.

Here is the Nixon view, as quoted from his book, *Leaders*: "The essential qualities of any successful leader are that he enjoy power, will strive to gain it, and, once lost, struggle to regain it."

Sam Ervin's definition describes it this way: "A leader wants power not for himself but in order to be of service. I think a good leader exercises power to improve the lot of other people or to improve a system."

During our interview, Sam Ervin hinted that his insights didn't just come out of nowhere. He often spent the better part of a Saturday or Sunday sitting in his Morganton office in front of a legal pad, minting one simple definition. Many of these have become law or have been printed the next day by newspapers from coast to coast.

When you read this interview, you will notice a subtle difference between it and all the others. This is a man who has nothing to sell but dedication to the truth.

A SIMPLE COUNTRY LAWYER?

"Adversity is the diamond dust with which life polishes its jewels," explains former Senator Sam Ervin Jr. in an exclusive interview with Personal Selling Power.

To many Americans, Senator Ervin is that storytelling, Bible-quoting, folksy moralist who gave Nixon advisors an eye-opening cram course on integrity when he presided over the televised Watergate hearings in 1972.

But to people close to him, he is an illuminating, self-directed man with keen insights into human behavior. His great knowledge of law and history have equipped him to meet the challenges of adversity countless times.

His persuasive logic helped end the McCarthy era in the 1950s.

His love for the Constitution and his country earned him the status of a modern-day link to the founding fathers.

Senator Ervin shares the techniques that have helped him to judge people, to influence people, and to present his arguments clearly and convincingly.

Although he retired from the Senate in 1973, he still works between eight and ten hours a day in his modern and cheerful Morganton law office. His enthusiasm is contagious. His detailed recall is impressive. Only a more cautious step testifies to his age. He'll soon be eighty-eight—and is still going strong.

PSP: You once suggested that two books should be in the White House at all times. One is the Constitution of the United States **and the other is Dale Carnegie's book,** How to Win Friends and Influence People. **Why did you suggest that?**

Ervin: Well, I'll tell you. This was after a press conference where President Nixon said he had to impound funds because Congress was financially irresponsible. I thought that insulting Congress and charging them with the sole responsibility was a poor way to get their approval for his programs.

PSP: Do you feel that Dale Carnegie's book is still necessary in the White House today?

Ervin: Yes.

PSP: What are some of the ideas that you've learned from this book?

Ervin: There is a story in there of this old black man who always had such a good disposition. When somebody asked him what his secret was, he answered, "I've just learned to cooperate with the inevitable."

You know, a lot of us don't like to cooperate with the inevitable, and we get ourselves all worked up over things we cannot do anything about.

PSP: You've influenced many people in your career, and you have a great deal of insight into human behavior. How did you learn this?

Ervin: Well, I had a very good teacher, Henry Horace Williams. He said the things that try people's souls do not consist of choosing between good and evil. That's fairly simple. But the thing that tries a man's soul is having to choose between conflicting loyalties. That's the hardest thing you'll ever have to do.

For example, he used to say that every individual could be compared to a small dot in the middle of many concentric circles. He said the circles next to you would represent your loyalty to your family, your wife or your children, your church, your political party, or your country.

That concept has not only helped me in making better decisions, but I think it has helped me to judge other people more fairly. A lot of people have made choices that I thought were unwise, but when I stopped to analyze these, I thought that they were making choices between conflicting loyalties.

PSP: If you would use yourself as an example, what would be your number one loyalty?

Ervin: Let me give you an instance. A lot of times I just couldn't support measures advocated by Democratic presidents. I felt that my controlling loyalty was for my country, and I voted for what I thought was best for my country, rather than for a congressional party. If the Republicans made a good proposal, I supported it.

You see, an English writer said once about the House of Commons in England that the timid members of the House of Commons all too often think about the security of their seats, rather than the security of their country.

PSP: How do you know which loyalty should be number one?

Ervin: We all find occasions where we have to choose between what we believe is right and what we suspect is advantageous. And this is quite a conflict. For example, in public office the first thing you have to do is to be satisfied about the rightness of your views; secondly, you need to be industrious and do whatever work and study is necessary to reach a sound and honest conclusion. Third, you need to have the courage to stand up for that conclusion, regardless of whether it is popular or not.

PSP: Would you say then that if you've searched for the truth and if you've chosen your loyalties, you have developed a sound platform upon which you're going to be more persuasive?

Ervin: That's right! Especially in a legislative office where you're constantly trying to persuade people to accept your views.

PSP: Could we take this loyalty model and apply it to the profession of selling?

Ervin: All right.

PSP: In selling, we have three concentric circles. We have the customer, the salesperson, and the company. The company needs sales, the salesperson needs success, and the customer needs satisfaction. How would you choose between conflicting loyalties if you were the salesperson?

Ervin: Well, I have the conviction that if you want to make a convincing argument for whatever you're selling, you need to be convinced that your product is good. Next, you need to be genuinely interested in your profession. You want to satisfy yourself in making a success and achieving something in selling your product. On the other hand, I think a salesperson gets a lot of satisfaction from the knowledge that the customer is going to be satisfied with him or her.

Right along that line, Squibb Pharmaceuticals used to

have a little slogan that I loved. They said, in every compound, "The priceless ingredient is the honor and the integrity of the maker."

PSP: How do you define the word integrity?

Ervin: In my mind, it means the absolute fidelity to the truth. It's the quality that makes a person faithful to the truth. I think a lot of people yield to the temptation to make claims for products they know are false.

PSP: Could you give me an example?

Ervin: I used to be visited by a number of law book salesmen. One would come in and he would tell me that I had been fooled by buying these other books. He claimed that they were not worth a nickel. Well, I thought that statement was a reflection on my intelligence, and it certainly wasn't calculated to win friends.

I bought almost all my law books from another salesman. He would come in with a book and show me how it would unlock the secrets of any of the books I already had.

PSP: He sold you on the benefits of his books?

Ervin: Right. But the other salesman did not lose only that one sale. He lost his chance of repeat sales, he didn't get any leads, and he damaged his company's image or good will.

The definition of *good will* is the inclination of satisfied customers to return to a merchant for further trade. I think, in the long run, honesty is the best policy.

PSP: How would you define ethics?

Ervin: The purpose of ethics is to encourage you to live in such a way that when you lie down at night, you can sleep without any misgivings about what you've done.

PSP: Have you ever lied?

Ervin: Well, I don't know. My father used to say he didn't know whether a person could live the life of a Christian gentleman without lying occasionally. I guess sometimes out of sincerity we say some nice things to people— more than they deserve. But I don't think that's a very bad habit, because most people need encouragement to get through this troublesome world.

PSP: *Is it ethical, in your opinion, to persuade other people to do what you want them to do?*

Ervin: Yes, if you are trying to persuade them to do the right thing.

PSP: *Let's say you know that another product is doing the same thing but it is cheaper than yours. Would it be ethical to persuade others to buy the more expensive product?*

Ervin: It would, in a way, because there are products that may be more expensive but are more satisfactory to own. A lot of people take a lot of pleasure out of owning something that is more expensive than other folks'.

PSP: *Could we discuss some of the techniques that you've used in your career to persuade others and to present your ideas convincingly?*

Ervin: All right.

PSP: *It appears that you are using stories, analogies, and sometimes even poetry to sell your point of view.*

Ervin: Yes, I've always liked poetry. In the first place, it is the most beautiful way of expressing anything, because it is music in words. Secondly, a poet has the capacity to express an exceedingly profound truth that nobody can really deny in just a few words.

PSP: *So, instead of your furnishing evidence to support your arguments, you recite a poem or use an analogy and leave the other party with the responsibility of picking it apart.*

Ervin: That's right. It's impossible; they can't argue with it.

PSP: *You once used an analogy to accuse the Chief Justices of committing verbicide on the language of the Constitution. I've never heard the word verbicide.*

Ervin: I'll tell you where I got that word. Oliver Wendell Holmes' father was a physician in Boston. He coined that word by saying that there was a connection between the words *homicide* and *verbicide*. He said, "Verbicide is a violent treatment of a word with fatal consequences."

PSP: So, instead of accusing the Chief Justices of not telling the truth . . .

Ervin: I've accused the Supreme Court of being guilty of verbicide, twisting the words of the Constitution to mean something that it didn't mean.

PSP: You also use a great many stories to illustrate your points. How did you develop this technique?

Ervin: My father always loved to tell stories. He was a lawyer for sixty-five years in North Carolina. I used to practice with him in the mountain counties. Well, it took us many hours to get to these county seats, so when the lawyers and judge got there they stayed there all week. They had nothing to do at night except to sit around and tell stories. I accumulated a lot of stories that way.

PSP: Could you give an illustration of how a story has helped you sell your point of view more effectively?

Ervin: For example, they had a bill to prohibit the teaching of evolution in the schools of North Carolina back in 1925. The fundamentalists were in favor of that bill, and I always figured that a little humorous story can sometimes help to kill a bill.

I first told them that the bill would be an attempt to set limits on the boundaries of human thought, which was impossible.

But, secondly, I said, "I have to admit I am opposed to the bill, although it will do one good thing. It will gratify the monkeys to know that the North Carolina legislature will absolve them from all responsibility for the conduct of mankind."

PSP: So, the outcome of the final decision was influenced by your use of humor?

Ervin: Yes. I've found that an ounce of humor will have more convincing weight than a ton of evidence.

PSP: You once used an aphorism by Thomas Carlyle, saying, "The first duty of a man is that of subduing fear." What was it that you feared most in life?

Ervin: I didn't give this too much thought. Joanne Bailey wrote a little poem that said, "Courage is not an absence of fear, but the ability to overcome or disregard fear."

PSP: How do you overcome fear?

Ervin: I've heard that Robert E. Lee wrote to his son when he was admitted as a cadet at West Point, "I think that fidelity to duty is one of the best ways of overcoming fear." I feel if you've got a commitment to something, then you do what you've got to do.

Fear has been the most devastating enemy of mankind of all ages. The alternative to your fear is that you've got to realize that many of the things you fear have never happened and never will happen. And, even if they were going to happen, the alternative may be even worse.

I remember a radio announcer, almost a generation ago, commenting on the fear of atomic war. He said, "Atomic war would be awful; biological war would be worse; but there is something worse than either one and that is subjection to a foreign oppressor."

PSP: Two years ago, you wrote a book entitled **The Whole Truth about Watergate.** *This was shortly after President Nixon published his memoirs.*

Ervin: I don't think I would have ever written it if it hadn't been for his memoirs.

PSP: Now, there is a new book written by Richard Nixon, entitled **Leaders.**

Ervin: Yes, I know.

PSP: In this book, he talks about the essential qualities of a successful leader.

Ervin: Well, I was reading in the paper that he was on one of the morning shows to justify lying, and according to him it was sometimes necessary to practice hypocrisy to win political battles.

PSP: Here is a quote from **The Wall Street Journal** *saying, "An essential quality of any successful leader in the Nixon view is that he enjoys power." How would you define leadership?*

Ervin: Nixon talks about power. He wanted power for Dick Nixon. A person who is worthy of being a leader wants power not for himself but in order to be of service.

PSP: So, good leadership is . . .

Ervin: I think a good leader exercises power to improve the lot of other people or to improve a system.

PSP: So, good leadership can be measured by how much the leader can improve the lives of other people.

Ervin: Yes. Also, a good leader has to have a good knowledge of history. I had a high admiration for Truman. He didn't have much formal education, but he knew history.

I always like the expression of an English historian, James Froude. He said, "History is a voice, forever sounding across the centuries, the laws of right and wrong." If I were the dictator of the United States, I'd have one requirement that nobody could finish high school without studying history. History is a light; it's the lamp of truth. Any country that ignores the lessons that history teaches is doomed to repeat the mistakes of the past.

PSP: How would you like to be remembered?

Ervin: I don't want to be a memory too soon. I would like to be remembered for two things—first, for fighting to preserve Constitutional government and, second, for fighting to preserve the rights of individuals.

PSP: What's your measure of success in life?

Ervin: My father always used little aphorisms. He said, "An idle brain is the devil's workshop." I think that the most satisfaction we get out of life is the realization that we've done our job and we've done it to the best of our ability.

HOW TO INFLUENCE PEOPLE

Techniques of Persuasion Used by Senator Sam J. Ervin Jr.

The appropriate story Robert Kennedy wrote in his book, *The Enemy Within,* "I heard Senator Ervin on several occasions destroy a witness by telling an appropriate story which made the point better than an hour-long speech or a day of questioning."

For example, during the McCarthy hearings, he influenced other senators with this tale:

A young lawyer went to an old lawyer for advice as to how to try a lawsuit. The old lawyer said, "If the evidence is against you, talk about the law. If the law is against you, talk about the evidence."

The young lawyer said, "But what do you do when both the evidence and the law are against you?"

"In that event," said the old lawyer, "give somebody hell. That will distract the attention of the judge and the jury from the weakness of your case."

Humor "I can't imagine how a person gets through life," said Senator Sam Ervin, "takes the rough licks he gets, without a sense of humor."

For example, in a debate about school prayers, he cited a quote from Chief Justice Stacy of the North Carolina Supreme Court:

" . . . Men have gone to war and cut each other's throats, because they could not agree as to what was to become of them after their throats were cut."

Here is another humorous tale Senator Ervin loves to share:

There was this man who was known as the most ignorant man in Burke County, North Carolina. Somebody once asked him if he knew what country he lived in, and he an-

swered flat out, "Nope." They asked him if he knew the name of the state, and he again answered, "Nope." Well, they then asked if he had ever heard of Jesus Christ. "No," he answered. Finally, they asked if he had ever heard of God. "I believe I have," he said. "Is his last name Damn?"

Analogies Sam Ervin spent countless hours of concentrated thought searching for effective analogies to illustrate his points.

Analogies are illuminating persuasive tools designed to show how different situations correspond in certain ways. We could call them mental link trainers.

For example, when President Ford pardoned former President Nixon, Senator Ervin did not tell the press that he did not approve of the pardoning. He used this analogy instead:

I have said all along the pardoning power of the president is greater than the pardoning power of the Almighty. The Almighty can't pardon anyone unless they repent. The president can pardon anybody, even if they deny they ever committed any sin.

In an article in *U.S. News and World Report,* he defended the integrity of Congress with this analogy:

If one public official goes wrong, too many people lump all of them together. If one red-headed man robs a bank, we should not conclude that all red-headed people are bank-robbers.

In another instance, he explains the absurdity of one man's thinking:

He resembles the man who put vitamins in his liquor, so he would build himself up while he was tearing himself down.

Definitions Presenting a sharper image of a common thought is Sam Ervin's specialty. He confessed that he was inspired by Oliver Wendell Holmes, who wrote:

A word is not a crystal, transparent and unchanged; it is the skin of a living thought that may vary greatly in color and content according to the circumstances in which it is used.

During a speech at the University of North Carolina, Senator Ervin encouraged students with:

The world of the mind is an illimitable land whose boundaries are as vast as the universe itself, and thought is calling us at all times to the undiscovered countries lying beyond the next visible range of mountains.

In a record entitled *Senator Sam at Home* (Columbia), he defines the meaning of the words *defeat* and *faith*:

Defeat may serve as well as victory to shake the soul and let the glory out.

Faith lets us walk in those areas outside the boundaries of human thought.

Aphorisms Sam Ervin's aphorisms could become a devastating weapon in the courtroom or in public debates in Congress. During the famous Watergate hearings, he quoted Shakespeare's Henry VIII to lecture an all too eager White House aide:

Had I but served my God with half the zeal I served my King, he would not in mine age have left me naked to mine enemies.

Other Ervin favorites are:

Power corrupts, and absolute power corrupts absolutely. (Lord Acton)

Necessity is the plea for every infringement of human freedom. It's the argument of tyrants; it is the creed of slaves. (William Pitt The Younger)

What's right is right and what's wrong is wrong. You can't compromise with integrity.

*An organization that wants a place in history has no need
for a shredder.*

Poems "It's difficult for others to disagree with a
poem," explains Senator Sam Ervin.

He frequently uses poems to get the attention of his
audience and persuade them to yield to a new line of
reasoning.

> *I have to live with myself*
> *and so, I want to be fit*
> *for myself to know,*
> *I want to be able as*
> *days go by,*
> *always to look myself*
> *straight in the eye.*
> *I don't want to stand*
> *with the setting sun,*
> *and hate myself for*
> *the things I've done.*
>
> *Edgar Guest*

On many occasions, he gently persuaded others to avoid
rambling and to come to the point by reciting Longfellow's
"A Psalm of Life:"

> *Art is long*
> *and time is fleeting.*
> *And our hearts, though*
> *stout and brave.*
> *Still, like muffled drums,*
> *are beating funeral marches*
> *to the grave.*

SENATOR SAM J. ERVIN JR: KEY IDEAS TO REMEMBER

1. Integrity is the quality that makes a person faithful to the truth.

2. The thing that tries a man's soul is having to choose between conflicting loyalties.

3. We all find occasions where we have to choose between what we believe is right and what we suspect is advantageous.

4. A good leader exercises power to improve the lot of other people or to improve a system.

5. An ounce of humor has more convincing weight than a ton of evidence.

Now please complete the Action Plan on the following page.

MY ACTION PLAN FOR SUCCESS

1.

2.

3.

4.

5.

11

Portrait of Communication:

ART LINKLETTER

When most people think of Art Linkletter, they recall his popular TV show, "People Are Funny," and see a mental picture of a grown man squatting next to a child and getting that child to say the most innocent and at the same time outrageous things.

Since I didn't grow up in this country, I never saw that legendary show. But when I studied Suzy Sutton's interview with Art Linkletter, I was in awe—in awe of a system that produces these marvelous and heartwarming stories of success, seemingly out of the blue. I became aware that there was more than a cultural system at work. Art Linkletter himself had taken what that system had to offer and combined it with his own personal philosophy to create great success in his life.

At the heart of this man's life work is communication. Perhaps the toughest job in entertainment is the task of the master of ceremonies, the MC, whose role is to get others to perform. And if you can do that, and especially if you can make children act like themselves in all their glorious innocence, then you are simply a master communicator.

Art Linkletter discovered early in his show-business career that getting other people to be themselves provided the most entertaining show in the world. His success in his later life has revolved around those early lessons with people onstage.

The key to good communication for Art Linkletter is in listening, looking, and feeling how the other person feels. It involves enjoying the moment and working within it to achieve success. Those people who always see success as something down the road will always miss the success that is staring them in the face. Art Linkletter learned that by staring into thousands of eyes, by reading the faces of all kinds of people, and, most important, by communicating openly and freely with them.

Communicating and persuading go hand in hand. You cannot persuade someone if you fail to listen. And you can't become a Superachiever if you can't communicate.

It is Art Linkletter who reminded me that our ability to talk only amounts to 49 percent of the communicator's job. The remaining 51 percent needs to be spent listening. I found this idea to be of great help in selling whatever the product might be. No one ever listened himself or herself out of a sale.

AN INNER VIEW OF AN INNER WINNER

Arthur Gordon Linkletter, whose face is as familiar to most Americans as their favorite breakfast cereal, can look back on a life filled with one success after another, as entertainer, author, businessman, and public speaker.

But Art Linkletter is looking ahead, not back, and he sees a future of absolutely endless opportunities. In this exclusive interview with Personal Selling Power, *he tells us how to make the most of the opportunities to come in the next ten years. He's so excited about the prospects that he would like to face them at twenty years of age without a quarter in his pocket!*

PSP: We all know that you're an enthusiastic advocate of the free enterprise system. How did you get that way? Why?

Linkletter: Because I started with nothing, and I was given the opportunity to get everything through work and perseverance, planning and goal setting, not forgetting the spur of adversity. So I must, of course, be an enthusiast for any system that permits an unknown, unnamed, abandoned orphan to get to the top of the heap. And that's what this system does.

PSP: When did you first know that you wanted to be a professional speaker, a salesman of ideas and ideals?

Linkletter: I suppose that it started when I was eleven or twelve years of age. I was getting ready to go to Woodrow Wilson Junior High School, which was being built in east San Diego. Following the regular school day when the workmen had left the building of the auditorium (the seats were unfinished, empty), I used to go over and stand on the stage and make pretend speeches to pretend audiences. But it wasn't really until I got into college and started studying to be an English professor, when I began to work in debating, speaking, and writing that I realized where my heart really lay.

PSP: You've achieved great success, and you are a role model for so many people. Do you attribute this success partially to luck, or to what?

Linkletter: Luck comes when opportunity meets preparation. But timing is important, too, and I happened to come along at a marvelous time. In 1933, with the invention of radio came the invention of the "man on the street" show. And when I heard that, I said, "Now, there is something I can do!"

PSP: And you soon became an American institution and later expanded into TV. How did you get into the speaking profession?

Linkletter: In a sense, I'd always wanted to speak, and I'd always been a speaker at informal appearances before service clubs and at rallies to raise money for hospitals and charitable causes. But it was only in the last twelve or thirteen years that I became what might be called a professional lecturer. And it arose out of free appearances that I made as a memorial to my daughter, who had died during a drug incident, and I was speaking against drug abuse. I embarked, partly at the behest of Norman Vincent Peale, on a crusade to try to save young people. And it was during this time that I really began to spread my wings. Talking about drug abuse led me into talking about human frailties of all kinds and the need for positive, motivated living.

PSP: You've been talking a great deal on how to win over the many adversities that come with a rapidly changing world. Do you think that in spite of the many external changes, the individual is totally responsible for his or her life?

Linkletter: Oh, yes. In fact, I speak about that quite often. The real answer to getting people off drugs, vandalism, sex orgies, or all the other destructive things lies in personal responsibility. You must take charge of your own life, and you must not point the finger at luck, fate, other people, or your family history. You can say that you've had problems because of these other things, but ultimately you are responsible for yourself. I tell people that they must develop a healthy self-esteem. They must think enough of themselves to invest the extra vigilance required to meet all new challenges head on.

PSP: You are a man who appears to have a very high regard for human beings. To what do you attribute your high degree of self-esteem, in spite of all the obstacles and barriers you've encountered?

Linkletter: I've worked with young people all my life. I started out wanting to be a YMCA secretary because my parents were old people when they adopted me. My father was crippled; he was unable to play games with me. He was a strict and stern Baptist minister, so I didn't have the freedom that other young people had. The YMCA became, in a sense, my foster father. I became a leader in youth work and later a schoolteacher; then, because of circumstances, a radio announcer. I think working with young people gives you a special flavor of energy, inspiration, and joy.

PSP: I can see that you have preserved this special flavor.

Linkletter: I think too many grownups forget the child inside them. That's the important thing. All of us have a child inside of us who's spontaneous, curious, happy, carefree, mischievous, and all the other kinds of pretend things that children are. People think that maturity and adulthood preclude the ability to enjoy that part of our lives. So they turn it off; they cover it up. I encourage it to come out. It leads to more honest, more successful relationships.

PSP: You mention success. What does it mean to you?

Linkletter: I would think that success is the hardest word in Webster's dictionary to properly define because it's so personal. It has so many different meanings for each person. We're all motivated by different inner drives.

My own definition is doing what I like to do best and doing it better all the time. In my opinion, success is a journey, not a destination. So, if you're successful in your travel toward success, that becomes success.

PSP: Abraham Maslow coined a term called peak experience. He mentioned that successful people can feel this special sensation many times in their lives. Can you tell us about this from your own journeys toward success?

Linkletter: I would say that an incident occurred recently at a very large meeting of establishment people who are of the Fortune 500 group. I was speaking to them about the free enterprise system and where it was going, and I gave such a glowing report with my philosophy of America today and in the next twenty years that the audience was electrified. I could get them up out of their seats with a turn of a phrase or even a raised eyebrow. At the end, I had three or four minutes of a standing ovation from people who are ordinarily a bit slow to express that kind of enthusiasm because they're chief executive officers and they have the aloofness characteristic of top command.

PSP: You have always had a great ability to sell people on our free enterprise system. What do you envision for the next ten years?

Linkletter: I think a very important book for anybody to read these days is Alvin Toffler's *The Third Wave.* It is one of the most interesting books I have ever read in my whole life. In the third wave, we're going to see the standard, old-fashioned, large industrial complexes (steel, rubber, automobile, and things like that) give way to what Toffler calls "the cottage civilization." which means that more people are going to be working in smaller units, in their homes in many cases, with computer controls and data analyzers and the input from where you're actually best suited to live.

PSP: Isn't that going to narrow our perspective?

Linkletter: No, I don't think so. The wider a choice you have, the more people are going to be tempted to experiment. And it will be slow growth; it won't be revolutionary.

PSP: Then, what you're saying is that people need to expand their awareness of their choices in order to grow.

Linkletter: Right. I would love to be twenty years of age, without a quarter, facing the next ten years, because I think the opportunities are absolutely endless.

PSP: But most people don't think so! They're wailing and weeping that it's all been said and it's all been done. And here you're saying, "This is just the beginning."

Linkletter: Oh, just the beginning. There are so many opportunities today, so many chances, that I weep at people who say it's all been said or done. It hasn't. We've just started. And many of the things need to be resaid and redone better. There's a whole new generation waiting, anxious and eager and, I think, hungry for all kinds of new experiences. I also think that some of the standards have been lowered in the last fifteen years so that people of quality, determination, and perseverance stand out like lighthouses. In a time when people want to get along and go along, the people who are forging along and forging ahead are just that much more quickly recognized and rewarded.

PSP: *Would you say that you are fulfilling whatever purpose you think you have in life?*

Linkletter: I am now. I think that for many years I was doing something that was great fun and I think brought a lot of entertainment to people and made me a lot of money, but I was purely a selfish person, driven toward getting rich and famous. And that, I suppose, is not too abnormal in the world of entertainment. But I think in the last fifteen years my life has broadened out, and I see much more clearly the good I can do and the constructive things I can give. Because the more you give, the more you get. And my life has really been in three phases for almost seventy years.

The first was the struggle of a poor boy in the Depression. The second was the giddy, unnatural, unbelievable wealth and fame and power that comes with this business we're in. And then the third came from the realization of maturity that you should give back the things that you get.

PSP: *From what you're saying, and the way that you look right at this moment, you're enjoying this third phase more than the other two.*

Linkletter: Oh, much, much more. In every way!

PERSUADING BY PAYING ATTENTION

By Art Linkletter*

I suppose one key to my success as an interviewer in radio and TV has been sympathetic, encouraging, thoughtful listening. Some interviewers, instead of thinking about what their guest is saying, spend the time thinking up a wisecrack or another question. So their interviews go nowhere.

Most people being interviewed feel insecure, children

---

*Excerpted from the book *How to Be a . . . Supersalesman,* by Arthur Gordon Linkletter, Copyright ©1974, by Arthur Gordon Linkletter. Published by Prentice-Hall, Inc., Englewood Cliffs, N.J.

most of all. Take a five-year-old and put him in front of lights and cameras and a big audience of strangers; what are the chances of getting him to say much? Almost nil. But I found that by looking him in the eye unwaveringly, never glancing around, never seeming amused or shocked, never demeaning his replies no matter how ridiculous, always staying on his level—by doing all this I virtually hypnotized him, narrowing his focus of attention to me exclusively so that he talked naturally. I realized that if I could do this with a child, I could do it with adults. Try it.

ART LINKLETTER: KEY IDEAS TO REMEMBER

1. Success is a journey, not a destination, so, if you're successful in your travel toward success, that becomes success.

2. You must take charge of your own life, and you must not point the finger at luck, fate, other people, or your family history. You can say that you've had problems because of these things, but ultimately you are responsible for yourself.

3. Luck comes when opportunity meets preparation.

4. There are so many opportunities today, so many chances, that I weep at people who say it's all been said or done. It hasn't. We've just started.

5. I see much more clearly the good I can do and the constructive things I can give. Because the more you give, the more you get.

Now please complete the Action Plan on the following page.

MY ACTION PLAN FOR SUCCESS

1.

2.

3.

4.

5.

12

Portrait of Greatness:

DR. DENIS WAITLEY

"When I experience pain," explains Dr. Denis Waitley, "I now view it simply as a signal for change. It tells me that I either need to change the way I do things or change the way I look at things."

During the interview, we spoke at length about his work with athletes and the psychology of winning. Athletes, it seems, must first be able to understand the meaning of pain before they can go on to the task of winning.

For most people, this is a difficult concept. We are all aware of pain in our lives, and we live in a society eager to kill pain the very moment it occurs. Some people are so frightened of even the possibility of pain that they tend to avoid many of the challenges that could bring success to their lives.

Dr. Waitley's philosophy of viewing pain as a signal to change led to his own personal growth and success.

"There are two kinds of pain," he explains. "The first is the pain that comes from within and is self-inflicted; the second comes from the outside and is largely beyond our control."

He speculates that 80 percent of all pain we experience in life is of our own creation and, therefore, manageable and useful, while 20 percent is created by external circumstances beyond our control.

Using this philosophy, Dr. Waitley has helped world-class athletes to overcome physical pain by seeing it in a different framework. The change of mental focus initiated by pain becomes part of the motivation to succeed. Pain becomes the signal that success is just around the corner.

Dr. Denis Waitley's early life was a study in frustrated goals. He thought he wanted to become an astronaut. When he couldn't achieve that, he felt he was a failure. It wasn't until he saw that his goal was not defined based on his personal philosophy of success (but was based on his father's) that he began to use the pain as a signal to grow beyond his impossible dreams.

He realized that people constantly mourn the loss of their impossible dreams, which brings them self-inflicted pain. Identifying and giving up the impossible dreams and focusing on truly self-created goals is the only way to achieve success in any field.

Dr. Waitley did not take charge of his life until he was age thirty-five. At that point he realized that the starting point to success can only be reached through self-awareness, self-knowledge, and a self-created philosophy of success. He quickly outgrew his goal of becoming an astronaut, thus stopping the self-inflicted pain, and became a Superachiever who reached a level of success that far exceeded his initial dreams.

Dr. Waitley helped me realize that there is no growth without meeting pain. Although growing is painful, it is more painful not to grow. What's even more interesting, he has taught me to respond to pain first by seeking solutions and not to react to pain by killing it unexamined.

PLANTING THE SEEDS OF GREATNESS

Dr. Denis Waitley is a national authority on high-level performance and personal development. He holds a doctorate in human behavior and currently serves as a visiting scholar at the University of Southern California College of Continuing Education. Dr. Waitley serves as a consultant to major corporations and to government and private organizations on behavior modification, goal setting, and morale enhancement.

Dr. Waitley is the author of the all-time best-selling audio cassette album, The Psychology of Winning. *Surprisingly, the text of this cassette program was written, as Dr.*

Waitley revealed in this candid interview, at a time when he was experiencing the "reality of failing." He recently introduced his latest book, The Seeds of Greatness.

PSP: You have studied the success patterns of some of the greatest achievers around the world. What are the three most common characteristics these winners share?

Dr. Waitley: The first would be high self-esteem, the feeling of your own worth. The second, the realization that you have the responsibility for choosing your own destiny. The healthiest, most successful people I've seen exercise their privilege to choose. The power of choosing their destinies puts them in charge of their lives. The third characteristic would be creative imagination to translate dreams into specific goals.

PSP: What is your definition of a winner?

Dr. Waitley: A winner is, in my opinion, an individual who is progressively pursuing and having some success at reaching a goal that he or she has set for himself or herself; a goal that is attained for the benefit, rather than at the expense, of others.

PSP: In doing the research for our interview, I found that there are more than 220 books that deal with the subject of winning and only sixteen that deal with the subject of losing. Do you think that there is an overemphasis on winning?

Dr. Waitley: The idea of winning has been misunderstood and overexposed. It's associated with flying through airports, driving fast cars, or standing over a fallen adversary. I've seen salesmen and saleswomen who were making six-figure incomes, thinking that they had won. They thought winning was reaching a certain financial level or getting to a certain point. Thinking they have arrived, they stand still and go to the country club. Now their company expects more production but won't get it from them because they had the wrong idea. They didn't realize that winning is a continual process of improvement.

PSP: In 1976, two researchers, Thomas Tutko and William Bruns, published a book entitled Winning Is Everything *and Other American Myths. They wrote, "Winning, in fact, is like drinking salt water; it will never quench your thirst. It is an insatiable greed. There are never enough victories, never enough championships or records. If we win, we take another gulp and have even greater fantasies."[1]*

Dr. Waitley: It is true. The American version of winning is to come in first at all costs, or expediency rather than integrity.

PSP: Are you saying that people tend to get obsessed with winning at the expense of fulfillment?

Dr. Waitley: Definitely. I think athletics is the most dominant of all fields where payoff only comes to the winner, but there are notable exceptions. For example, in interviews with the five U.S. former Olympic decathlon winners, I found that their goal was to become the best they could, not necessarily the best in the world. These athletes have found fulfillment in recognizing and in realizing their potentials.

PSP: Their gold medals are internal, not external.

Dr. Waitley: Exactly. The secret is to compare yourself against a standard that you have set. You measure yourself only against your last performance, not against another individual's.

PSP: What is your definition of a loser?

Dr. Waitley: A loser is a person who has an abundance of opportunities to learn, who has successful role models everywhere, but who chooses not to try. I read the other day that only 10 percent of all American adults will ever buy or read a book. This means that 90 percent choose not to take advantage of the tremendous opportunities available to everyone in this country. Our libraries are crammed full with enough information for anyone to be an expert in anything.

PSP: Do you feel salespeople don't read enough?

Dr. Waitley: To me, the person who chooses not to read is more of a loser than the person who cannot read. I am not suggesting you need to be an intellectual in order to sell; I am just suggesting that if you want to move up, you definitely need the additional vocabulary.

PSP: You wrote in your book The Winner's Edge, *"Real success in life has no relationship to a gifted birth, talent, or IQ." Would you include gender?*

Dr. Waitley: Yes, and I would include race as well.

PSP: Whether you are a saleswoman or a salesman, it doesn't make a difference?

Dr. Waitley: It doesn't make a difference. In fact, there are advantages to both.

PSP: Where do you see the edge a woman has in selling?

Dr. Waitley: A woman has the edge of being more gifted earlier in the area of verbal communication. She has a better grasp of nonverbal signals, and she is able to show more empathy in recognizing customer needs. Women are more process-oriented. Society, however, has positively conditioned a man to believe that the world is his oyster, and he's been taught to risk in order to get rewards. Women have been taught to seek security. I think women need to be more risk-oriented to create security. I also think that men need to learn how to listen more before taking risks.

PSP: You have analyzed many winners. I wonder how we can ever know objectively how and why winners win.

Dr. Waitley: I don't think we can put it into a formula. But we can study people who have overcome obstacles in their paths. I studied people from every walk of life, like hostages, POWs, astronauts, sports figures, and sales achievers, to see if they have anything in common. There are surprising similarities.

PSP: Let me rephrase my question. Look at history. The country who wins the war gets to write the history books. History becomes the tale of the winner. If you translate this to people, winners get to tell their stories in interviews. Winners are the most inter-viewed people in this country. Do you think that they give us an objective picture? Is high performance an objective science or speculative science?

Dr. Waitley: It's a speculative science. But instead of comparing their methods on achieving success, we need to compare patterns of achievement and see how those pat-terns overlap. Also, we need to review their thoughts and actions during their worst times. Personally, I've learned more from the worst times than I have from the best mo-ments of my life.

PSP: Do you suggest that the strength of winners often depends on how they manage disappointment?

Dr. Waitley: Absolutely. When I studied the ad-versities faced by leaders like Anwar Sadat, Abraham Lin-coln, Walt Disney, Thomas A. Edison, and Golda Meir, I learned much more than by analyzing some of the great statements or decisions they made. When winners stand on the pedestal, they tend to gloss over what it took to get from the dream to reality.

PSP: Why?

Dr. Waitley: It's a human tendency to gloss over the difficulties and remember only the great breakthroughs. Many sales executives focus on the gloss and overlook the real opportunities.

PSP: How can we learn from our disappoint-ments in a way that enhances our growth?

Dr. Waitley: Most people never go beyond the adoles-cent view of failure. They say, "If they laugh at me, it isn't worth learning from the experience." Adolescents tend to believe that performance is the same as the performer. They take individual achievements as marks of their own self-esteem. The healthy individual views failure as a tem-porary setback. The stumbling block becomes the stepping stone. A better example would be the kid who got new ice skates for Christmas. He goes out on the ice and falls on his head. His mother comforts him by saying, "Why don't you come in and put your skates away?" and he says, "Mom, I didn't get my skates to fail with; I got my skates to learn with. What I'll do is keep practicing until I know how to do it right."

PSP: Disappointments seem to lead up to a choice between seeking comfort and seeking solutions.

Dr. Waitley: Exactly.

PSP: We are reluctant to grow and seek solutions because it's painful.

Dr. Waitley: Right. Eighty percent of all people view growing pain as too uncomfortable or unacceptable. Only 20 percent recognize it as a learning experience.

PSP: Could you give us an example of people who view pain as a learning experience?

Dr. Waitley: Well, during the 1980 Olympics I worked with the Australian rowers. The problem was that they experienced muscle spasms near the finish line. The coach told me that when they got from a sixty stroke-per-minute cadence up to sixty-four strokes a minute, the pain was nearly unbearable. It appeared like a no-win situation. So we developed an appreciation and understanding for the process of pain as being a growth experience. Pain tells you that the muscles are working and also that you are in the peak performance mode, which means that you are on your way to victory. We made the interesting discovery that the mind will block the pain as long as there is a positive expectation. By recognizing pain as being their friend, they ended the race without muscle spasms and they improved their performance significantly. Their minds, motivated by positive expectations, released powerful endorphins that killed the pain.

PSP: In your latest book, **The Seeds of Greatness,** *you suggest that the so-called motivators preach too much about attitudes without linking them with apti-*

tudes. What if you have great dreams for winning and a high tolerance for pain, but lack the basic talents to realize those dreams?

Dr. Waitley: I was cautioned by my friends, Dr. Jonas Salk and Hans Selye, not to tell people that they could walk on water. Why build up gigantic expectations in people without knowing what their real talents are? To shorten the answer, and I said this in the book, we now have specific and reliable tests available to assess thirty-two areas of natural, basic talents. Like the ability to carry a tune or the ability to put tweezers together on a minute object.

PSP: Who conducts these tests?

Dr. Waitley: There is a nonprofit organization, the Johnson–O'Connor Research Foundation, a human engineering laboratory with offices in major cities throughout the United States. They are headquartered in New York City.

PSP: Your father did not seem to have an appreciation of your talents when he expected you to become an Annapolis graduate.

Dr. Waitley: He appreciated my talents but tried to apply them to his own dreams. I wanted to write the great American novel and ended up as a carrier-based attack jet pilot.

PSP: So, you are saying that before people can reach their true potential, they need to discover their true talents?

Dr. Waitley: Yes. In my seminars, I ask the audience if they could live their lives over again, what would they do. Eighty percent of them say that they would be doing something else.

PSP: In your book, **The Winner's Edge,** *you said, "I didn't realize until I was thirty-five that I am behind the wheel in my life."*

Dr. Waitley: That's right.

PSP: What made you aware of that?

Dr. Waitley: I was failing a lot up until thirty-five.

PSP: At what were you failing?

Dr. Waitley: I became a good Navy pilot, but I never became the astronaut that I wanted to be. That, to me, was a failure. I could fly a plane, but I didn't get to fly a spaceship. Later, as a business executive, I earned an income but never retained any money. I had a couple of business failures. I fixed the blame on my father's suggestion to go to the Naval Academy. I rationalized, what can an ex-Navy pilot do except fly for an airline?

PSP: You thought that your opportunities were limited?

Dr. Waitley: Yes. Then I figured that I had never learned anything about money. I know a lot about words, so I took several staff positions. I began to see myself as a jack-of-all-trades and a master of none. People told me, "Denis, you are one of the most gifted, talented, creative, wonderful individuals we ever met. We are sure sorry you have not been able to convert that to financial or any other lasting success." At thirty-five, I probably was at the lowest point in my life. I had been traveling all the time. I didn't have a good family life. My resume looked like *Who's That?* instead of *Who's Who,* and I was actually believing that I might be born to lose—like my dad, because he never made any money either. Interestingly enough, and I don't think he would mind my saying this, a best-selling author today, a friend of mine, said as we were walking on the beach that he had the same experience. Until he realized that his dreams had substance, and until he started simulating success and being around people who were successful, he was destined, as was I, to have permanent potential. Now his book has been on *The New York Times* best-seller list for nearly a year.

PSP: What is his name?

Dr. Waitley: Spencer Johnson, the co-author of *The One-Minute Manager.*

PSP: So you walked on the beach, wondering if your dreams were realistic or not?

Dr. Waitley: Some of my dreams were pipe dreams. Becoming an astronaut was unrealistic. I recognized that these unattainable dreams led to repeated failures.

PSP: What did you do to get out of this failure pattern?

Dr. Waitley: I happened to get fed up with the repeating cycle. I began to seek shelter under the shade of winners. I got tired of running with the turkeys. The first thing I did was to find a very strong clergyman. I needed some real fatherly advice. We did go up 10,000 feet in an airplane. He knew flying was a comfortable environment, a success pattern for me. As we were going through the stalls and spins, he gave me reassurance and spiritual dimension at a time when I needed it most. The second thing I did was start going to seminars conducted by high-powered professionals who talked about stress, health, and success. I was studying their patterns of success. I got excited that maybe I was going to be acceptable in this kind of company. When things were at their worst, I began to write *The Psychology of Winning.*

PSP: So at the lowest point of your life, you actually created the biggest sales hit in the cassette market. How did your program get published?

Dr. Waitley: I think Earl Nightingale and Lloyd Conant are the only two who know this, but after I'd finished *The Psychology of Winning,* I took my last $500 and flew to Chicago. At that time I was speaking in churches, getting less than $50 a speech. Someone who believed in me had sent a single cassette that I'd recorded in church to Earl Nightingale. He called me and told me that he liked my voice and thought I had some good ideas. He said if I was ever in Chicago, I should see his partner, Lloyd Conant. I went on the next airplane, and Lloyd Conant believed in my work enough to help me polish up my initial draft and took a chance on recording *The Psychology of Winning,* which literally converted me from almost total anonymity to a certain measure of success.

PSP: Now that you've met with success, do you feel an overabundance of success can spoil us?

Dr. Waitley: Absolutely. If you put the roar of the approving crowd, the amount of money you make, and the material accomplishments into a bag and say that is success, you would be making a big mistake.

PSP: What are the danger signals of success? When do you know that you are not riding success but success is riding you?

Dr. Waitley: There are several telltale signals. Number one, an obsession to talk about your own accomplishments all the time. Two, whenever people tell you something about what they did, you top them. The third thing is an obsession with your own material rewards. A tendency to show them more. You invite people to see the monuments that you've collected.

PSP: In your new book you are suggesting that trying to collect life is a self-defeating proposition.

Dr. Waitley: Yes. We can't collect life; we can only celebrate life.

PSP: But if we examine your journey to success, we could say that before we can celebrate, we need to manage our disappointments.

Dr. Waitley: I really believe so. We've got to view failures and rejections as healthy experiences from which to grow. We've got to replace someday fantasies with goals that we can really track and chip away at every day. We've got to let go of our impossible dreams and stop putting happiness and success on layaway.

PSP: I'd like to share an interesting quote with you. Abraham Zaleznik wrote in a Harvard Business Review article entitled "The Management of Disappointment," that "There is irony in all of human experience. The deepest irony of all is to discover that one has been mourning losses that were never sustained and yearning for a past that never existed, while ignoring one's own real capabilities for shaping the present."[2]

Dr. Waitley: That is really profound and is said so well. Because planting the seeds of greatness means investing your natural talents in the pursuit of realistic goals. Not every seed will grow into a flower, so you need to view these failures as learning experiences. But to enjoy the flowers in your garden, you have to pluck the weeds. This means that you have to recognize and give up your pipe dreams.

PSP: And if you don't?

Dr. Waitley: Your natural seeds of greatness will never have an opportunity to bloom.

Notes

1. Copyright © 1976 by Thomas Tutko and William Bruns. Used with the permission of Macmillan Publishing Company, New York, N.Y.

2. Copyright © 1967 by the President and Fellows of Harvard College; all rights reserved. Reprinted by permission of the *Harvard Business Review* (Nov.–Dec. 1967, Vol. 45, No. 6).

DR. DENIS WAITLEY: KEY IDEAS TO REMEMBER

1. A winner is an individual who is progressively pursuing a goal that he or she has set for himself or herself, a goal that is attained for the benefit rather than at the expense of others.

2. A loser is a person who has an abundance of opportunities to learn, who has successful role models everywhere, but who chooses not to try.

3. The strength of winners often depends on how they manage disappointment.

4. Eighty percent of all people view the pain of growing as too uncomfortable or unacceptable. Only 20 percent recognize it as a learning experience. Don't react to pain by killing it unexamined; learn to respond by seeking solutions.

5. Recognize and give up your pipe dreams. Invest your natural talents in the pursuit of realistic goals.

Now please complete the Action Plan on the following page.

MY ACTION PLAN FOR SUCCESS

1.

2.

3.

4.

5.

13

Portrait of Positive Thinking:

DR. NORMAN VINCENT PEALE

"Not a day goes by that I don't have a struggle to overcome negative thinking," explained Dr. Norman Vincent Peale in our interview conducted at his impressive Fifth Avenue office in New York. "How do you think I learned so much about positive thinking?" He smiled at me as he admitted that he was "the most negative thinker in the world."

The commitment to turn negative thinking around to positive thinking has become Dr. Peale's guiding philosophy.

I found a man who long ago had the sense to choose a positive-thinking wife, a man who has realized the value of being open to every facet of life. His openness is not only disarming but also keeps a constant stream of positive experiences flowing through his entire life.

As we talked, I felt a deep sense of respect and felt I was smart to take the advice of this sage. He helped me realize that every single problem in life contains its own solution. All we have to do is find ways to open the problem and extract the solution. Thus, his classic line: "A problem is nothing but concentrated opportunity."

His unique ways of dealing with everyday problems and his advice have been a godsend to millions of people. He has taught the meaning of faith through his words and his actions. It takes only a little imagination to follow his logic when he says, "The only thing stronger than fear is faith."

His wisdom brought back Senator Sam Ervin Jr.'s quote: "Faith lets us walk in those areas outside the boundaries of human thought."

No matter what your religious beliefs are, Dr. Peale's concepts and philosophies have been successful for too long to be brushed aside without putting them to the test in real life.

In spite of his worldwide popularity, Dr. Peale's positive thinking has not always found enthusiastic acceptance. In my research I was told of a story that was attributed to the late governor of Illinois, Adlai Stevenson. Many years ago, Dr. Peale wrote a very positive and enthusiastic account of Paul the Apostle's life. When Stevenson was asked what he thought about Dr. Peale's latest work, he quipped, "I always found Paul appealing, but I find Peale appalling."

I realize that the world cannot be cleared of negative thinkers or cynical people, but I am convinced that we can make it a better place by starting with our own minds.

THINKING POSITIVE

For millions of people throughout the world, Dr. Norman Vincent Peale is The Power of Positive Thinking, *his famous book which has become one of the top best-sellers of all time in more than thirty languages.*

In this exclusive interview with Personal Selling Power, *Dr. Peale tells how positive thinking can be the power behind a successful salesperson. He also discusses the attitudes that lead to sales success, the techniques of positive imagination, the energy drain of negative thoughts, and how to deal with the two common factors of failure.*

Dr. Peale, called the most influential Protestant clergyman in the United States, has gained enduring fame as pastor of Marble Collegiate Church since 1932, author of numerous best-selling books, editor of Guideposts *magazine, and radio and television commentator. His distinguished career began more than sixty years ago in Ohio when he took a job as a door-to-door salesman.*

PSP: Is it true that you've been in the business of selling pots and pans?

Dr. Peale: That is right, and I think I am still in the selling business. I see salesmanship as a process of persuasion whereby another individual is induced to walk the road of agreement with you. If I persuade you that this chair is what you want and you agree, then you walk the road of agreement with me and you buy it. The same is true when I am in the pulpit. If I give you a concept that is going to be beneficial to you and you accept it, I have sold it to you, even if you do not have to pay me any money for it.

PSP: *You said once that many people fail in selling because they are victims of a "hardening of their thoughts and attitudes." What kind of attitudes lead to sales success?*

Dr. Peale: Let's say you're coming to sell me life insurance. You know that in order to buy groceries and clothes for your family, you need to sell so much insurance. Now, if you come in with that attitude, then you convey to me—maybe unconsciously—that I've got to buy insurance from you to help you out, to do something for you. However, if you believe that you are going to help me by offering the protection, the financial security, and the benefits of working with your company, that positive attitude is very likely to result in my signing the order.

PSP: *You once defined the word* personality *as "how you affect or stimulate others and how others affect or stimulate you." How do you prevent a customer's negative attitude from stimulating you negatively?*

Dr. Peale: I was reading in the newspaper the other day that President Reagan was going to have a meeting with a South American president. He was told by his worried aides that this president was going to give a speech criticizing the United States. Reagan just leaned back and said with a smile, "Well, we'll smother him with love." Now, I do not particularly like the word *smother,* but when you've got a difficult customer, the thing to do is to send out good will thoughts, love thoughts, understanding thoughts, and remain at all costs dispassionate. Just take a scientific attitude and ask yourself, "Why does he act that way?

There must be something disturbing him that I don't know about."

PSP: *It's not because of you that he's acting that way.*

Dr. Peale: That's right. So, you love him just the same. It's nothing personal. You just take him as he is and like him.

PSP: *Instead of wishing he were different.*

Dr. Peale: You can't make him over. You expose a pleasant nature to him and take him as he is.

PSP: *So, your own attitude remains positive.*

Dr. Peale: Right.

PSP: *You've recently written about positive imagination. How can your techniques be used in selling?*

Dr. Peale: There is a deep tendency in our human nature to become ultimately almost precisely what we imagine or image ourselves as being. A customer may say, "That is very interesting, but I don't need your merchandise right now. However, I will keep this in mind." Keeping it in mind means that the customer will hold the image of a later purchase. Cultivation of an image is very important in selling.

PSP: *Images plant the seeds.*

Dr. Peale: That is a good figure. Seeds will flower. While you are busy planting, you are imaging the flowers. That is the image. When you buy seeds, you are sold by the picture of flowers on the package. Images do the selling job for you to a considerable extent.

PSP: *Do you think that our images and thoughts are mainly responsible for how we feel?*

Dr. Peale: You can make yourself sick with your thoughts, and you can make yourself well with them.

PSP: *So, if you think negative thoughts, you're creating negative emotions which in turn drain your energy?*

Dr. Peale: Definitely. The negative emotion creates tiredness, which takes energy and vitality out of you. A positive emotion is created by positive thoughts and images. You can say, "This is a great day. I am fortunate to sell a wonderful product. I look forward to meeting many interesting people today. I'll be able to help some of these people and they will become my friends. I look forward to learning a great deal today." Thinking and talking that way adds to your enthusiasm and vitality. Your mind is expanding, and all this contributes to your well-being.

PSP: On the other hand, you could start with 100 percent energy at nine o'clock in the morning and reach a 30 percent level at noon by engaging in negative thinking.

Dr. Peale: Yes, you can completely wear yourself out by the debilitating quality of your thoughts.

PSP: In other words, positive thinking maintains the original energy you already have.

Dr. Peale: If you think positively, hopefully, optimistically, enjoyably, pleasantly, then your words will have a therapeutic effect. If you put yourself down mentally, you are reducing the vitality of your system. I knew a doctor once who told me of a man who actually killed himself by hate thoughts.

PSP: Why is it that people can't resist thinking negative thoughts to the point of hurting themselves? It is because they can't stop thinking these negative thoughts, or is it because they cannot imagine positive thoughts?

Dr. Peale: It requires strength of character to make the transition to a positive thinker. It isn't easy. When a person is born, he or she is a positive thinker. I've never seen a negative baby. But a baby may be born into a home where perhaps one of the parents is a negative thinker. He or she may listen to negative teachers, or he or she may be surrounded by negative friends. If that person desires to be a positive thinker, he or she faces a complete reversal of mental attitude. That person will have to gradually reorganize his or her mind and develop new tracks across the brain. This may take some time. Some people think they can read a book and all of a sudden become positive thinkers.

PSP: What would be the starting point to achieve this positive change?

Dr. Peale: Well, the realization that you are not right in your mental attitudes and that you must change would be the starting point.

PSP: So, awareness would be the first step. What would be the second?

Dr. Peale: The commitment to begin practicing positive thoughts. You can develop any mental habit if you're convinced that it will lead you to success and happiness in life. Then, you commit yourself to it and hang in there and stick with it and never give it up.

PSP: Mrs. Peale wrote in her book, The Adventure of Being a Wife, *which is a wonderful book, "I think he writes about positive thinking because he understands so much about negative thinking."*

Dr. Peale: That's right. She knows me quite well. I was indeed a negative thinker, the worst you could imagine. I had little faith in myself and thought that I was a failure. This was until one of my professors told me that I had a choice—that I could think positive thoughts and stop thinking negative thoughts, and that this choice would determine my future.

PSP: Are you still having negative thoughts?

Dr. Peale: Sure, I have negative thoughts.

PSP: Could you give us one example?

Dr. Peale: Well, yesterday was Sunday. I had to go to the church to preach a sermon. When my wife and I arrived in our garage, the attendant said, "Dr. Peale, I've got bad news for you. Your car won't start." So I took a look at it. I got in and indeed it wouldn't start. So we decided to take a taxi. Now, this morning my wife asked, "What are we going to do about the car? We've got to go upstate tomorrow and the car isn't operating."

I said, "I don't know what we are going to do. There is no mechanic in the garage, and if we call a mechanic from the outside he will show up next week." Here was a negative thought from the person who wrote the book, *The Power of Positive Thinking.*

So she said, "Let's believe that we're going to get that car fixed today," and she is right now with the mechanic getting it repaired. It is a good thing to have a positive-thinking wife.

PSP: How can you increase your level of awareness of negative thoughts entering your mind?

Dr. Peale: I figure that I am the sovereign judge of any thought that goes through my mind. Remember the old saying, "You can't stop the birds from flying over your head, but you can keep them from building a nest in your hair." If a negative thought comes to your mind, you sit as judge with sovereign power over that thought, and you can let it stay there and grow or you can cast it out. By practicing positive thinking as long as I have—being basically negative—I have developed the ability to throw out the negative thought quickly. The moment my wife said we were going to fix that car today, I agreed and ejected the negative thoughts.

PSP: You seem to propose only two choices— negative thinking and positive thinking. What about realistic thinking?

Dr. Peale: The trouble is that what most people think is realistic is actually pessimistic. Look at the way newspapers write about reality. It's mostly negative. You don't find many positive thinkers in newspapers, because news is a departure from the norm. They only write about bad things that happen.

PSP: Newspapers don't write about the human potential.

Dr. Peale: There are very few positive publications. Our magazine, *Guideposts,* is one of the positive periodicals.

PSP: In a recent speech, you talked about the two common factors leading to failure—inertia and aimlessness. How do you propose to deal with these?

Dr. Peale: Inertia is a difficult one. Another name for it is just plain downright laziness. It is a habit, growing in an unenthusiastic, depressed attitude of mind. Once you get into the habit of action, you'll create more enthusiastic thoughts by which to rule out inertia. Action creates motivation. Action is the best medicine I know.

**POSITIVE
THOUGHTS**
1000 mg.

J. DOE
Sales Representative
Take 3 times daily

Dr. Norman Vincent Peale

Positive Attitude Laboratories

PSP: How about aimlessness?

Dr. Peale: If you want to avoid failure, you must develop sharp, clearly defined, enthusiastic goals. Something you want to attain. I recently talked to John Johnson, the publisher of *Ebony* magazine. He was very poor and started that magazine with $600 borrowed from his grandmother. He decided he wanted to be a publisher and set small, attainable goals, one after another. Now, he not only has *Ebony* but other magazines as well. The little goals were the starting point, but way out ahead he had a big goal. He could see it. He imaged it.

PSP: How about the problems on your way to your goals?

Dr. Peale: A problem is a concentrated opportunity. The only people that I ever have known to have no problems are in the cemetery. The more problems you have, the more alive you are. Every problem contains the seeds of its own solution. I often say, when the Lord wants to give you the greatest value in this world, he doesn't wrap it in a sophisticated package and hand it to you on a silver platter. He is too subtle, too adroit for that. He takes this big value and buries it at the heart of a big, tough problem. How he must watch with delight when you've got what it takes to break that problem apart and find at its heart what the Bible calls "the pearl of great price." Everybody I've ever known who succeeded in a big way in this life has done so by breaking problems apart and finding the value that was there.

PSP: In your book, The Power of Positive Thinking, *you mention a study saying that 75 percent of the people surveyed listed as their most difficult problem the lack of self-confidence. Do you think that is still true today?*

Dr. Peale: Yes, there are so many people who have no confidence. They don't believe in themselves.

PSP: Your wife wrote in her book, "Norman's creativity carried a price tag, and that price tag was a constant vulnerability to self-doubt." How did you overcome it?

Dr. Peale: I haven't overcome it. I still wonder whether I can put this speech across, and so I say to myself, "Do you know this subject?" And I say, "Yes, I've studied it." Then I say to myself, "There is Bill Jones out there in the audience, and he's going to listen to me and he thinks I know something that will benefit him." So, I begin to fortify my self-confidence, because of Bill Jones's faith in me. I say a prayer and then I say to myself, "Forget yourself, forget your name, don't make a big deal out of this; simply go out there, love those people, and help them."

PSP: It's like with selling. You could say, "Forget about yourself, and talk about your customer's needs."

Dr. Peale: That's right. Go in there and help that customer. I tell you, I think that life is a battle from the beginning to the end. One of the biggest battles you will ever have will be with yourself.

PSP: Victory over yourself seems to be the goal.

Dr. Peale: That's goal number one. Even if it takes you ninety years and you win victories, the old enemy of self-doubt sneaks up at you again and you must continue to hit him again, knock him out, and go forward. There is only one mental pattern that is stronger than fear, and that is faith. So, cultivate faith and that will be your substitution for self-doubt.

PSP: You've said recently, "American people are so nervous and high-strung that it almost makes it impossible to put them to sleep with a sermon." How do you combat stress without sacrificing success?

Dr. Peale: Stress comes from tension, worry, and anxiety. You can quiet yourself down if you just deepen your faith in God, in people, in yourself, and in the power of love.

PSP: If you throw a blanket of faith over a personal problem, isn't there a possibility of covering up something that prevents you from growing?

Dr. Peale: Of course, that is always a possibility. To me, a positive thinker is a rugged soul who sees every difficulty. But he is not defeated by them because he knows that he has within his own mind the ability to understand, to define, to make judgments, and to arrive at right decisions. In addition, he has what it takes to overcome, to live with, or to reduce the problem. In a sense, he is a realist in that he sees everything straight, but is never overawed by difficulty.

PSP: *What is your meaning of success?*

Dr. Peale: The meaning of success, in my judgment, is to be a whole person—completely in charge of yourself. It is to be someone who sees life as a wonderful opportunity, someone who goes out to do the very best he or she can with a positive attitude. Now, if that means being a doctor where you work eighteen hours a day but you enjoy being a doctor, you love it—whether you make much money or not—you are still a success. Some of the wealthiest people I've known have been the most unsuccessful because they were filled with worry that they wouldn't keep their money, they didn't know how to use it . . .

PSP: *So, to you, success means doing the work you enjoy doing.*

Dr. Peale: Exactly. For me, it means writing books, running all over the country, making speeches . . .

PSP: *One hundred years from now, how would you like to be remembered?*

Dr. Peale: I'd like to be remembered as a person who helped people to be great persons.

HOW POSITIVE ARE YOU?

Answer each question below. Give yourself 10 points for each Yes answer and 0 points for each No answer. Add the totals.

Questions	Points
1. Have you had a stream of positive thoughts today?	☐
2. Have you smiled today—before you left home?	☐
3. Do you always maintain a positive attitude—even when you have to deal with negative people?	☐
4. Have you helped a client or prospect with a problem during the last three days?	☐
5. Have you read (or listened to) positive information during the past twenty-four hours?	☐
6. Do you have at this moment a clearly defined, enthusiastic goal?	☐
7. When you lose a sale, do you immediately continue building positive self-esteem?	☐
8. Do you sincerely believe that faith is stronger than fear?	☐
9. Have you planned for a positive, quiet moment for yourself today?	☐
10. Do you feel that each problem contains the seed to its own solution?	☐

TOTAL SCORE ☐

Total your score. A score of 100 means that you are 100 percent positive. The difference between your score and 100 indicates the amount of thinking required for a more positive you.

DR. NORMAN VINCENT PEALE: KEY IDEAS TO REMEMBER

1. You can make yourself sick with your thoughts, and you can make yourself well with them. Negative thoughts create negative emotions that take energy out of you. Positive thoughts and images create positive emotions and restore your energy.

2. You are the sovereign judge of any thought that goes through your mind. You can't stop the birds from flying over your head, but you can keep them from building a nest in your hair.

3. The only thing stronger than fear is faith.

4. A problem is a concentrated opportunity. The only people that I have ever known to have no problems are in the cemetery. Everybody I've ever known who succeeded in a big way in this life has done so by breaking problems apart and finding the values that were there.

5. Action creates motivation. Action is the best medicine I know.

Now please complete the Action Plan on the following page.

MY ACTION PLAN FOR SUCCESS

1.

2.

3.

4.

5.

14

The Interviewer's Insights

This book began with a simple reader survey on the subject of success. After the survey had been published, I realized the true meaning of Peter Drucker's saying, "The trouble with good ideas is that they quickly degenerate into hard work."

Seventeen months of preparation, research, interviewing, and editing have led to a closeup view of twelve Superachievers who have contributed more than 700 years of experience to this project.

The process has been enlightening for me. My wife tells me that I have gone through a chameleon-like process with each interview.

The amount of research involved for each one necessitated my spending hundreds of hours at the Library of Congress in Washington, D.C. It was during those hours, spent sifting through the mountains of material, that these interviews took shape.

It seems appropriate to say something about the Library of Congress here. The discovery of this place, for me, was nothing less than unbelievable. And it still remains one of the things about this country that I love most. The accessibility to ideas, to information, and to people—to me, the Library of Congress embodies all of that.

But what's more important, I enjoy that most marvelous atmosphere in a building that seems to say, from deep inside history, "We are all here, watching you, thinking with you, wondering with you. Together we can search for the answers."

When I researched under the subject heading of Success, I found more than 1200 books. Many of them present only a single point of view on the subject—the author's.

As the publisher of *Personal Selling Power,* I feel a responsibility to present a multitude of ideas. I see my publishing role as a broker of ideas between the reader and the people who have reached the pinnacle of success. In a sense, I create a platform from which Superachievers can present their unique points of view.

I did not conduct two of the interviews included here. Let me say a few words about the interviewer. Suzy Sutton is a professional speaker, and communications consultant to business and industry. She hosts her own talk show on WIOQ in Philadelphia and is superbly qualified in the art of interviewing. In this book, she is totally responsible for the interview with Art Linkletter. Her interview with Dr. David Burns was invaluable. In fact, I was so fascinated with the concepts he shared that I contacted Dr. Burns to customize the interview for our sales audience. I've learned a great deal from Suzy's interviewing style, and we are proud to count her as one of our contributing editors.

The first interview I conducted was with Zig Ziglar. It was an auspicious beginning and set the framework that would take me through all the others.

It is a strange phenomenon that when I researched each Superachiever, I began from a premise of doubt and suspicion. I was always looking for the conflicting ideas, the false statements, the come-ons. From there, I moved on in my mind to question where this person's ideas came from, what life experiences had molded his or her thinking. And at that point, without exception, a surprising thing happened. I felt that for a certain period of time I became a part of that person's mental universe. I began to see the world suddenly from his or her perspective, and I found that each person had discovered a basic truth. More than that, each Superachiever had found a concept that others could use to increase their life success.

After that, it was only a question of growth for me. When the time came to interview each Superachiever, I was ready. I had read every one of their books and studied the many articles that have been written about them or by them. I knew so much about their lives and their guiding philosophies that I could almost predict their answers to my questions. This preparation allowed me to devote my full attention during the interview to searching for previously uncharted areas. In many instances, I walked away with the impression of having contributed to the creation of new ideas.

The Superachiever's philosophies stayed with me long after the interview was completed. In the process of editing the final printed version, I managed to synthesize, for myself and for the reader, the essential guiding philosophies and success action steps outlined in this book. For months thereafter, I found myself reevaluating the thoughts or statements from each interview. I have come to incorporate many of these success ideas into my own life.

It was not my intention or objective to create exposés or unearth petty scandals. There are enough other people doing that every day. I was aiming, instead, at developing those ideas that could help other people, as well as myself, achieve a new level of success in all phases of life. To educate and motivate has been my goal.

We can learn much from the "sweat equity" of these Superachievers. I have tested their concepts and found them to be sound. I encourage you to do the same.

In conclusion, I have a final concern about the subject of success. Success in any area is not a panacea for life's problems. Success can be more transitory than love, more fleeting than a cloud. One success does not ensure the next. Success in one area does not exclude disappointing experiences in another. Success for Mary Kay could not prevent the death of the husband she loved. For Wayne Dyer, it could not prevent the pain of divorce and separation from his children. For Art Linkletter, it could not prevent the loss of his daughter in a drug incident. For Venita Van-Caspel, success could not ease her sorrow when her good friend recently died in an airplane tragedy, echoing the earlier tragedy and pain of her husband's death. Success cannot protect us from our basic human vulnerability. The human condition, no matter how successful, will always contain a mix of pain and pleasure. In many instances, success and failure are largely a matter of luck. But the realization that luck authors some of our successes and failures should not lead us to spend all of our energies on controlling fate and none on the pursuit of realistic goals.

All Superachievers invest their energies and efforts in areas they can influence and avoid investing in areas they can't control. In the end we must, as Senator Sam J. Ervin Jr. counseled, "accept the inevitable."

15

Success: The Magic Kingdom

Everyone wants it. Not enough of us feel we have it. There is no single definition of it. It eludes a great many of us.

Success, the magic kingdom, is always just beyond our grasp. The moment we feel it in our hands, it slips away. Fleeting and illusory, success is to some a feeling, to some a goal, to others a figure on the bottom line.

In the interviews with the Superachievers in this book, we came to realize that success, like love, is all things to all humans. Yet, in the final analysis we must all define it for ourselves. No one can convince a person who doesn't feel successful that he or she is a success. No one can define success for me or for you. Woody Allen once quipped, "Success is just showing up." And there's truth in that. For some, getting the job done is success. For others, success can only be claimed when the ultimate victory has been achieved.

On this, everyone is in agreement: One success leads to another. The self-perpetuating nature of success is a phenomenon matched only by the self-perpetuating nature of failure. Anyone can be caught in its web.

Success is not reserved for those of royal descent, for the rich, or for the powerful. All of the Superachievers in this book came from average backgrounds, and some came from the most difficult circumstances, overcoming great hardships to attain their success.

Success is always there waiting for you. Sometimes circumstances and fate conspire to toss a success your way. The prepared person, the one who is out there coping and not quitting, is the one who will be in position to catch the toss when the ball heads his or her way. If you drop one ball, another is certainly on the way.

The myth that success only comes your way once in a lifetime has been debunked by all of these interviews with Superachievers. Every one of them has known great failure long before great success. Every one of them has tasted the bitterness of defeat. But every one has resolved to try again. Every one discovered that to let defeat or failure in one instance cloud their life picture of themselves was to accept failure as a life mode.

Your own attitude about yourself in relation to the world says more about your success potential than anything else. Your expectation of how you will perform in any situation or set of circumstances will tell the world how well you will do. Success, contrary to what most people think, is not made up of the momentous decisions we make in life. It comes from the moment-to-moment life choices we make.

If I am on a diet and I want to be successful at losing weight, it doesn't matter what I eat three weeks from now. It matters what I eat today, right now, at this meal, for this snack. This is true for all decisions.

Attitude says more about how we are going to perform than words can ever tell.

For some, competition is the only road to success. Without feeling someone else's breath on their necks, these people would be napping by the side of the road. For others, competition has the opposite effect, making them want to hide in a safe harbor. Both types can function successfully when they position themselves in the right environment for their own success pattern. We learned from Mary Kay that competition can be hurtful and that everyone can be a winner without shoving someone else off the road.

There is a special quality in those people who have achieved success in life. Their relationships with others have a glow about them. There is a warmth in their presence. Success in relationships is the most difficult to attain. In searching for it, we lose it; in grasping for it, we find it slipping through our fingers. A butterfly is at its most beautiful when fluttering free on invisible currents of air. Pinned down on a board, its colors are magnificent and its shape is elegant, but it no longer fills us with wonder. The same is true of the baby first learning to walk. The baby takes a step, stumbles to his or her knees, then tries again, with wobbly knees and all the cuteness in the universe in the tiny struggle. To hold a baby in our arms forever is to deny the beauty of growth and independence.

Success in relationships is like that butterfly or that baby. We can only bask in their beauty, grace, and freedom. We cannot make them happen by will. The moments of delight cannot be extended or pinned down on a board. We can only let them happen in the climate of acceptance we have prepared.

The open-endedness of success in the relationships of our lives is wholly different from the success of winning a football game or being promoted to sales manager. To understand this difference is basic to achieving this success.

The Superachievers in this book understand that success and achievement are goals to work for. But they know that the real success is in knowing that the doing is more important than the result. The result will only be a reflection of the guiding philosophy, attitude, skill, and hard work that went into the end result.

The Dutch philosopher Spinoza once said, "No matter how thin you slice it, there always will be two sides." The closer we look at success, the clearer we can see both sides—the roots of success and the fruits of success.

The roots of success consist of your success philosophy, which grows out of self-knowledge. The fruits of success consist of what you want out of life.

Remember that everyone wants to enjoy the fruits of success, but only those who bother planting the roots will be able to harvest and enjoy the fruits.

16

Reference Guide to the Superachievers

**Following is a List of
80 Books By and About
the 12 Superachievers**

Mary Kay Ash

Mary Ash. New York: Harper and Row, 1981.
The Mary Kay Guide to Beauty. Reading, Mass.:
Addison-Wesley, 1983.

Dr. David D. Burns

Feeling Good: The New Mood Therapy. New York:
William Morrow, 1980, New York: Signet, 1981.

Dr. Kenneth H. Cooper

Aerobics. New York: M. Evans, 1968.
The New Aerobics. New York: M. Evans, 1970.
The Aerobic Way. New York: M. Evans, 1977.
The Aerobics Program for Total Well-Being. New
York: M. Evans, 1982.
Read also: *Aerobics for Women.* Mildred Cooper. New
York: M. Evans, 1972.

Dr. Wayne W. Dyer

Counseling Techniques That Work. Washington:
APGA Press, 1975.
Your Erroneous Zones. New York: Funk and
Wagnalls, 1976.
Pulling Your Own Strings. New York: Crowell Com-
pany, 1978.
Group Counseling for Personal Mastery. New York:
Sovereign Books, 1980.
The Sky's the Limit. New York: Simon and Schuster,
1980.
Gifts from Eykis. New York: Simon and Schuster,
1983.

Senator Sam J. Ervin Jr.

Role of the Supreme Court: Policymaker or Adjudicator? Washington: American Enterprise Institute for Public Policy Research, 1970.

Quotations from Chairman Sam. Edited by Herb Altman. New York: Harper and Row, 1973.

The Whole Truth. New York: Random House, 1980.

Humor of a Country Lawyer. Chapel Hill: University of North Carolina, 1983.

Read also: *Senator Sam Ervin's Best Stories.* Thad Stem. Durham, N.C.: Moore, 1973.

Just a Country Lawyer. Paul R. Clancy. Bloomington, Ind.: University Press, 1974.

A Good Man. Dick Dabney. Boston: Houghton Mifflin, 1976.

Art Linkletter

I Wish I'd Said That. Garden City, N.Y.: Doubleday, 1968.

Linkletter Down Under. Englewood Cliffs, N.J.: Prentice-Hall, 1968.

Drugs at My Door Step. Waco, Tex.: Word Books, 1973.

How to Be a . . . Supersalesman. Englewood Cliffs, N.J.: Prentice-Hall, 1974.

Women Are My Favorite People. Garden City, N.Y.: Doubleday, 1974.

200 Ways to Save on Probate, Inflation, Taxes and . . . Avoid the Financial Pit. Washington: Acropdis Books, 1977.

The New Kids Say the Darnedest Things. Boston: G. K. Hall, 1979.

Yes, You Can. New York: Simon & Schuster, 1979.

Hobo on the Way to Heaven. Elgin, Ill.: D. C. Cook, 1980.

I Didn't Do It Alone. Ottawa, Ill.: Caroline House, 1980.

Public Speaking for Private People. Indianapolis: Bobbs-Merrill, 1980.

My Child on Drugs? Cincinnati: Standard Publishing, 1981.

Linkletter on Dynamic Selling. Englewood Cliffs, N.J.: Prentice-Hall, 1982.

Gerard I. Nierenberg

How to Read a Person Like a Book. Coauthor: Henry H. Calero. New York: Hawthorn Books, 1971.

Fundamentals of Negotiating. New York: Hawthorn/ Dutton, 1973.

Meta-Talk. Coauthor: Henry H. Calero. New York: Cornerstone Library, 1973.

How to Give and Receive Advice. New York: New York Editorial Correspondents, 1975.

The Art of Creative Thinking. New York: Cornerstone Library, 1982.

Dr. Norman Vincent Peale

The Power of Positive Thinking. New York: Prentice-Hall, 1952.

The Power of Positive Thinking for Young People. New York: Prentice-Hall, 1954.

Stay Alive All Your Life. Englewood Cliffs, N.J.: Prentice-Hall, 1957.

The Amazing Results of Positive Thinking. Englewood Cliffs, N.J.: Prentice-Hall, 1959.

Sin, Sex, and Self-Control. Garden City, N.Y.: Doubleday, 1965.

Enthusiasm Makes the Difference. Englewood Cliffs, N.J.: Prentice-Hall 1967.

Norman Vincent Peale's Treasury of Courage and Confidence. Garden City, N.Y.: Doubleday, 1970.

Bible Stories. New York: Franklin Watts, 1973.

You Can If You Think You Can. Englewood Cliffs, N.J.: Prentice-Hall, 1974.

Positive Thinking for a Time Like This. Englewood Cliffs, N.J.: Prentice-Hall, 1975.

The Positive Principle Today. Englewood Cliffs, N.J.: Prentice-Hall, 1976.

The Story of Jesus. Norwalk, Conn.: C. R. Gibson, 1976.

The Joy of Living. Kansas City: Hallmark, 1977.

The New Art of Living. New York: Hawthorn Books, 1977.

The Positive Power of Jesus Christ. Wheaton, Ill.: Tyndale House, 1980.

You Can Have God's Help with Daily Problems. Pawling, N.Y.: Foundation for Christian Living, 1980.

Norman Vincent Peale's Treasury of Joy and Enthusiasm. Old Tappan, N.J.: F. H. Revell, 1981.

Dynamic Imaging. Old Tappan, N.J.: F. H. Revell, 1982.

Positive Imaging. Old Tappan, N.J.: F. H. Revell, 1982.

The Art of Real Happiness. Englewood Cliffs, N.J.: Prentice-Hall, 1983.

Ronald Reagan

The Creative Society. Edited by Frank Kiefer. New York: Devin-Adair, 1968.

I Goofed. Berkeley: Diablo Press, 1968.

The Quotable Ronald Reagan. Edited by Joseph R. Holmes. San Diego: JRH and Associates, 1975.

The Official Ronald Wilson Reagan Quote Book. St. Louis Park, Minn.: Chain-Pinkham Books, 1980.

I Hope You Are All Republicans. Edited by Alan S. Miller. Berkeley: Catalyst Press, 1981.

The Reagan Wit. Edited by Bill Adler. Aurora, Ill.: Caroline House, 1981.

Ronald Reagan Talks to America. Old Greenwich, Conn.: Devin-Adair, 1983.

There He Goes Again. Edited by Mark Green and Gail MacColl. New York: Pantheon Books, 1983.

A Time for Choosing. (Speeches 1961–1982) Chicago: Regnery Gateway, 1983.

Read also: *Sincerely, Ronald Reagan.* Helene Von Damm. Ottawa, Ill.: Green Hill, 1976.

Venita VanCaspel

Money Dynamics. Reston, Va.: Reston Publishing, 1975.

The New Money Dynamics. Reston, Va.: Reston Publishing, 1978.

Money Dynamics for the 1980s. Reston, Va.: Reston Publishing, 1980.

The Power of Money Dynamics. Reston, Va.: Reston Publishing, 1983.

Dr. Denis Waitley

The Psychology of Winning. Chicago: Nightingale Conant, 1979.

The Winner's Edge. New York: Times Books, 1980.

The Seeds of Greatness. Old Tappan, N.J.: F. H. Revell, 1983.

Zig Ziglar

See You at the Top. Gretna, La.: Pelican Publications, 1975.

Confessions of a Happy Christian. Gretna, La.: Pelican Publications, 1978.

Building Your Sales Career. Dallas: Ziglar Corporation, 1982.

Motivational Music Songbook. Dallas: Ziglar Corporation, 1982.